THYME FOR PROVENCE

Lavender, People and Places

Neal Atherton

Neal Atherton
French Travel Writer

INTRODUCTION TO THYME FOR PROVENCE

What is my second book about? The first – FIRST TIME WE SAW PARIS – told the story of a very reluctant traveller that somehow made it to the very southern Catalan region of France, endured the most terrible start to his first foray abroad but was immediately charmed by a small café in Perpignan. The rest is history, experiences that were enjoyed (and endured) by immersing himself in French culture and people.

I want to show you how we moved on to independent travel and first of all how we discovered Provence – a region of fragrant beauty and a warm and generous people. It was another culture shock for our English sensibilities but I want you to have a flavour of this amazing land and the people to be met on your travels. I hope to inspire you to visit this beautiful region and country. This is not designed to be a guidebook but if you want to follow in my footsteps then you are very welcome. They go in a wonderful direction. My wish though, is that you will discover your own treasured places and people and this book tells of the deepening of our love affair with French travel. Provence is a joy, please read on and imagine that you are there.

ALSO AVAILABLE ON AMAZON –

Kindle etc.. & Kindle Unlimited.   Also in Print.
Search : NEAL ATHERTON on Amazon

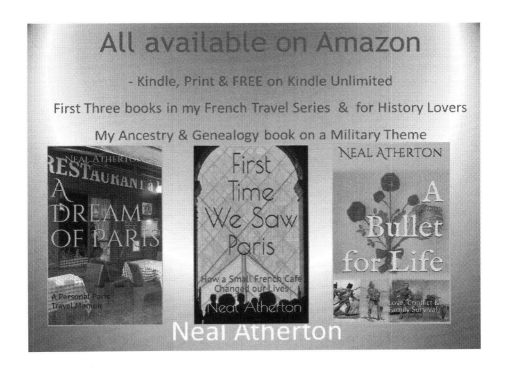

Best regards and thank you for reading, I very much

appreciate having you as a reader.

If you have any comments, feedback or wish to review
please go via my website :

www.nealatherton.com/contact-neal

or I am happy to be contacted directly.

Neal   Somerset   2019

nealatherton.com

THYME FOR PROVENCE

It was hot in the Luberon, temperature well into the high 80's and I found madam in the garden of this ancient house.

'Monsieur, vous êtes très chaud - you are hot from the journey, oui?'

I could only agree that I was indeed the very picture of the Englishman in the noonday sun.

She broke away from watering her extensive and beautiful enclosed garden.

'I will cool you down'

Turning the hose on my fully clothed self she most certainly did that.

Niamh called out as I returned up the stairs 'Did you get the correct key this time?'

She then saw me 'What......................?

So began a remarkable stay with the most free spirited of women in this incredible house.

It also gave us a flavour of the people and places we would find on our adventures in Provence.

This is the story of our travels in Provence and some of the remarkable people and places we have so fallen in love with.

A story of sublime meals and incredible scenery and villages, a story of happiness, laughter, tears of joy and frustration.

Enjoy our travels and please be inspired to discover this most beautiful of regions for yourself.

PEOPLE AND PLACES – EARLY RECOLLECTIONS

These are affectionate recollections and experiences from the early days of our independent travels to Provence. These are people and places that have shaped our travels and gave us the impetus to desire to get to know this region very well and we have never regretted any of our time spent in this beautiful area of France and our love of our travels here will clearly shine through.

This by necessity will be a longer chapter so I will break it up into sections around each interest point. I do hope that you enjoy reading about all that we have found and embraced in this wonderful region and most of all I trust you will want to visit Provence yourself and make your own story.

LOURMARIN AND THE VILLA SAINT LOUIS

In life you have your family and friends. You also gather many acquaintances who pass in and out of your life. The delightful joy and unpredictability of travel is that it occasionally throws up an opportunity to meet characters that although you will never really share your life with them or possibly even see them again they are ones you will never ever forget.

One of these people is Bernadette who owns the rambling Villa Saint Louis in Lourmarin.

Bernadette is the lady with the hose pipe that cooled me down in such style at the opening of this book and I most certainly will never forget her.

She is a woman who behind a high stone wall on the main street leading through Lourmarin inhabits a most astonishing 16th Century villa, she also undoubtedly inhabits a world that is most certainly her own.

Our three days at Villa Saint Louis were totally memorable for the personality and warmth of the lady, the quirky but very Provencal renovation of the house which seems to be a constant ongoing project, especially unforgettable however for her free spirited nature that you either had to run away from or simply embrace it. We choose to embrace it but I do have to say that was not always easy to do.

Niamh simply could not believe that she could have given me a cold shower in the manner she did. Nor indeed could I. But what could I do, for her it obviously seemed the natural thing to do and without having any prior warning I was defenceless. I was cooler it is true but a hot shower was what I really needed now.

This first meeting was light hearted if just a little, well actually, very surprising. The second encounter an hour or two later was not.

We had arrived at the Villa without any fresh fish or meat to prepare for the evening meal and so I wandered off down the narrow street into what passes for the centre of this small village in the hope of finding provisions. You may not be surprised to gather that I was unsuccessful as the only small store that was open had no fresh produce. They did have some frozen fish of dubious origin and species but as we were captive customers it was that or nothing.

Back at the Villa the solid rectangular block of reconstituted fish thawed quickly in the baking heat although food safety rules would probably want me to tell you not to try this at home. Part of the attraction in booking a room at this Villa was that although it was essentially a Bed and Breakfast it did also have a small kitchen available for the guests to use. It had an oven and a hob and pans and utensils so quite naturally I assumed they were there to use and not some quirky decorative culinary display. Wrong!

I had only been pan frying the fish in olive oil for about a minute when Madam came bounding up the stairs, tearing into the kitchen at speed all the while shouting:

'Pas des poisons, pas des poisons'.

Apparently she had a local bylaw that prohibited any fish cookery in the house – only she was aware of this prohibition.

She gazed straight at me from an uncomfortably short distance with a mad accusing stare and no further words were needed. The part cooked fish was despatched to a suitable municipal bin well away from the Villa and I now knew better for next time but there would never be a next time. This kitchen would not be used by me again.

We tucked in to an unfulfilling vegetarian feast that evening and went to bed hungry but unable to stop breaking into a cackle of laughter recalling the day we had just gone through.

Next morning we went along the winding corridors for breakfast on the terrace of the film set that is Villa Saint Louis. The terrace could be located in a tropical part of the French Provinces of a hundred or more years ago. The whole Villa gives off the air of a French private members club of the 19th century but being slowly brought up to date with quirky chic French furnishings. It is an extraordinary place.

Sat at the long solid wooden table on the terrace you feel totally private and secluded with no hint that you are actually in the most Anglicised or perhaps more correctly the most Americanised village in Provence. You have travelled many years back in time. The next completely unexpected thing comes when your morning tea is served to you by a young attractive Asian Indian boy who is clearly no more than 19 or 20 years old.

This place plays tricks with your head. We quietly ask him how he comes to find himself here so obviously far from home, his eyes betraying an evident sadness, homesickness perhaps, a sense of wonder and shock as if he has been beamed into this mystical place by mistake a la Star Trek fashion. We do not get a convincing reply, either he is a good politician or he is not comfortable in talking about his personal circumstances. This is high level people watching.

The house itself is simply unique, there is nothing else out there on our travels that I have come across that is close to it. As you enter the property below the veranda you go through a labyrinth of shaded passages that contain vast quantities of cut and drying lavender – the scent is heady, the floor scattered with lavender flowers. The garden is teeming with wildlife and domesticated animals of all sorts. The villa is adorned with objects and furniture that must represent Madams extensive travels but it is of course based on Parisian and French chic. It is an ongoing project, at the time of our visit it was still exuding quite a bit of faded charm but I think now some 15 years later Bernadette will have it just as she always envisioned. It is a place where I can imagine in her younger days she held some extraordinary parties that would have spilled out beyond the terrace and the spirit of such evenings would have wafted throughout Lourmarin into the early hours.

She is a remarkable host, unpredictable, lively despite her advancing years and unbridled in spirit. A charming host once you settle into the ambiance of the Villa and someone who is unforgettable.

Lourmarin itself is very much an ex-pat village and filled with English and American tourists and people who have settled in the commune over the years and to some extent it gives the appearance that the French are only there to be running the services.

Definitely don't let that put you off visiting this delightful village however as Lourmarin has much to offer.

At the time of our visit one of these reasons to enjoy the ambiance was the fine Restaurant L'Antiquaire where on another steaming hot day we had lunch following a morning visit to Val Joanis winery near Pertuis. This restaurant was tastefully fitted out and decorated, maybe with an eye for what the Americans and English think a Provencal restaurant looks like, with lovely crisp linen table settings.

The meal did not disappoint us and we had gently spiced curried salmon rilletes as starters and then a truly superb thick sea bass filet with finely sautéed Provencal vegetables with herbs. Definitely this was a food highlight so far in this region of fresh simple produce and we finished with a trio of desserts of crème brulee, sorbet and melon with tuille biscuits.

Having been served a full bottle of Val Joanis rosé wine rather than the 50cl we ordered we needed to wander the streets for a while before driving on to explore the region.

That obviously meant more wine tasting and we did indeed find a wine shop that had been recommended to us and located just near to the tourist office.

I really do wish that more shop staff in England would show just half the enthusiasm of the young man that we encountered in there amongst the wooden crates temptingly opened and displaying some fine wines. He took us enthusiastically and knowledgably through the selection on offer, French only of course, and would quite happily have discussed his wines for hours but eventually between us we came to a selection to take home – for the English winter as I had asked him to consider our dark winter days and which he thought most amusing.

We told him that on the next stop of our travels we were going to Burgundy and would buy more wine there.

'Bon courage' he smiled and I understood exactly what he meant and I would definitely be buying reliable favourites in Burgundy without handing my wallet over for someone's recommendations in that minefield of choice.

No visit to Lourmarin would be complete without a visit to the old chateau. Even without going inside you can still sit and stare and be impressed by this splendid Chateau that was constructed between the 12th and 16th Centuries. It was left in a trust to be a place for arts to flourish due to a legacy in 1925 by its industrialist owner who had a passion for history. It is still thriving for such a purpose today and has an impressive collection of art and objects and it is now fully restored.

Lourmarin was full of surprises and a place that is for us for many reasons - simply unforgettable.

VAISON LA ROMAIN

Our first stop  on our travels by car into Provence from the north, our entrance to the sun, has nearly always been in the town of Vaison la Romain. It is for that reason a location that is important to us in telling our story of travels in Provence. It is for us the Gateway to Provence.

We have always found Vaison to be a perfect lunch stop after a journey that has usually begun in Burgundy after an overnight stop at a hotel in the heart of French wine country. On top of the fact that Vaison does provide some excellent food for the weary traveller it is a spectacularly atmospheric and beautiful ancient Roman town to visit. The clue is very much in the name of course. The Romans loved it here too but I suspect they had to cook their own food. Vaison is one of the very best preserved of Roman built French towns, the town is a place where you can spend many hours and still not have scratched the surface of the interest it has

to offer. I do love my history.

Let me first of all tell a tale of one of our first visits, a lunch stop as we entered Provence and the beginning of our holiday:

Despite a fairly torturous AutoRoute journey from Lyon, all stop start traffic on the way, it was still only around noon when we parked the car in the large square in the modern part of Vaison. I say modern because the 'old town' is across the river but todays more modern part is actually where the majority of the Roman ruins are to be found. We were more than happy to have made such good time on the journey to get down as far as Vaison considering that we were travelling at the height of the tourist season. Vaison la Romain was to be our refreshment stop and it was already extremely busy. We headed down past the shops and restaurants towards the ancient Roman bridge connecting the two parts of the town over the Ouveze river. This bridge was built in the first century AD and it appears on first impressions to be a fairly simple arch construction but that does not disguise that this bridge is a truly astonishing architectural achievement. It has stayed firm even though it is in constant use right down to our day despite weathering the many dramatic floods that have swept down this valley throughout the centuries. We crossed over the bridge and of course lingered to admire the view both ways down the valley from the centre of the bridge, waiting our turn as people moved slowly away. The finest view of this historic bridge and its situation spanning the river and joining both sides of Vaison is to drive or walk a few hundred yards north and take in the scene looking back towards the town. It is a spectacular sight. As you cross to the other side it is worth stopping to look at the towering war memorial in front of you that is extremely impressive in that it almost appears to have been carved from the solid rock face. Walking slowly up the ancient cobbled narrow streets of the old town we searched up and down the maze of narrow passageways for a small restaurant that we had previously enjoyed a fine lunch but found it shuttered up, unusually closed at this busy time of year.

It was at this tiny unnamed restaurant serving just three metal tables spread out across the stone cobbles of an opening in the passageway that we had a surreal encounter with a group of American tour-

ists the previous year. It was peaceful and cool in this lovely shaded
spot, quiet and secluded, we were
just starting to enjoy a simple lunch
of Nicoise salad and a dish of lamb
cutlets placed in front of me. We
tried to eat this very pleasant lunch
and drink our carafe of chilled local Rosé wine but the
heavy conversation from our fellow diners was pre-
venting any possible enjoyment. Despite all of them
heartily tucking into their lunch, a couple of them
ironically enjoying a very rare steak, one of the party
of Californians was recounting at great length and in
precise gory detail the full technicolour facets of her
recent stomach operation. I assumed that as she had
recalled to all in earshot that it extended to a 5 hour
operation she would just give the edited highlights
and I also assumed that she must have been asleep
during the procedure – maybe she had it videoed.
She did not leave out any detail. I also assumed that
the others in the party gazing at their juicy red steak
would eventually change the subject. They did not.

I was under no illusions that if they continued
this subject any farther then I would throw up and
Niamh was going ever greener as our food was look-

ing at us like an enemy taunting us rather than a plate of tempting beauty and pleasure. Ultimately we had had enough. I asked very politely if they might just possibly please consider changing the subject until we had eaten. I explained that we English once anesthetised are more than happy not to be informed of what occurred and as long as all goes well there is nothing more we need to know but I appreciated they had a different take on the fascinations of surgery. They kindly agreed but I had put them out of their or should I say her stride and they spoke not a further word until I paid the bill and wandered off down the lane.

So then, back to our visit on this particular trip.

As we were not particularly pressed for time we did on this occasion carry on strolling around the narrow streets threading through the old town and after a while we came to a large terraced courtyard on the route back down to the ancient bridge and this turned out to be the Hostellerie Bellfroi. It gave the impression from the ambiance at the tables to be too good to walk past and we would in any case rather eat in the old town with its extra atmosphere and views. One snag today that countered this argument was that the mistral wind was blowing hard, very hard and it turned out to be a bracing lunch on the exposed terrace. Even the wine bottle had to be 'grounded' such was the strength of the wind. I kept it by MY foot.

The food that the restaurant served was excellent and I enjoyed the plat du jour of roast chicken with Provencal courgettes with a side dish of boulangere potatoes. Niamh had a large salad of couscous, prawns and raisins with plenty of 'greens'. The splendid local Vaucluse Rosé was the finest of accompaniments once I could steady it to pour.

Clafoutis is always one of our favourite French desserts and we cook it often at home from a Normandy recipe so we both decided on the Apricot version that was on offer to finish a very pleasant lunch. Niamh insisted that hers was strangely 'chicken' flavoured. Maybe they had carried 'Plat du jour' a little too far with that one. Mine was absolutely the finest example of apricot flavour so we swapped over and I had the full chicken lunch. Niamh was indeed correct, it did taste of chicken, presumably warmed up TOO close to the next main course to be served.

The hotel restaurant waiting staff were quite young and seemed a little diffident as I observed that on a couple of occasions they lost lunchtime custom simply because of turning parties of six or so away until one large party took it into their own hands and showed them how easy it was to put tables together. After that they seemed to warm to their task and were pleasant and friendly, if a little inattentive.

As with most restaurants in France and particularly ones with a large terrace there is always scope for some excellent people watching, a skill you start to perfect after a few visits, and this place certainly does not disappoint on that score. At the next table under an old knarled shady tree I observe a scene that is replayed so many times as you eat your way around France. It is the ageing well preserved Frenchman, greying hair still luxurious and worn long and swept back, skin textured by the sun and Gitanes over the years but still retaining a certain Gallic attractive elegance and dressed in the finest clothes, new ones of course, large expensive watch on his bronzed wrist. At his side the young, very attractive girl, from the interplay between them she is definitely not his daughter or granddaughter it must be said, she is hanging onto his every fascinating word and while he expounds his philosophy on life and love he desires that his iPhone does not offer up a call from his wife.

Overall it was a fine tasty lunch in a lovely courtyard with a great view back over to the other side of the river. It is too early in our trip to make too many superlatives in our admiration with regard to views because there will as the week progresses be some stunning ones to come that are truly breath-taking and we will find many of these away from the main tourist 'must see' sights.

We will eat often over the coming years in Vaison on our driving tours around Provence.

So then, other than food what has Vaison to recommend it?

The old town offers the most delightful views either back across the river to the old town or looking in both directions down the valley and as you gain height in the old town to the very top the views increase in splendour. The actual top is quite rocky and a bit of a disappointment but at least it has not been turned into a tacky tourist place. As we near the top we hear the strains of an unusual stringed instrument. This zither like instrument is being played by the most bizarre musician, a middle aged man who has the appearance of a Biblical shepherd, enhanced by his long hair that I cannot imagine is his own, it looks like it started life on the back of a sheep. This long matted hair (wig) is extraordinary.

We leave him to his small crowd of admirers and retrace our steps as the piercing high notes fade into the distance. The buildings on this side of town are old and well maintained with many Bed and Breakfast establishments and Gites. Other houses are still occupied by local people and it is this mix that makes it such an interesting place to stroll.  The unexpected is around every corner, perhaps an elegant hotel with their diners on the terrace and then beyond that the washing line of the local lady resident.

It is up in the more modern half of Vaison that you will find the Roman ruins. They are ruins of course but are actually so well preserved that you need to engage very little imagination to visualise the town as it would have been laid out in Roman times. There is an admission charge for the two main sites but particularly with the large section of Roman town that is near the main square and leading over to the Cathedral you can walk around the perimeter and get a great free view looking down over the grid of ancient streets.

Some buildings are visually so obvious in their reason for having being constructed, the most amusing one is the large square room with solid stone benches around all the walls. These have circular holes cut into them at regular intervals and it needs no imagination to grasp that these were the Roman equivalent of the toilet pods on today's French streets. To be honest some of the toilets on the AutoRoute and in some rural cafes have not progressed very far in technological terms from these splendid practical examples from Roman times. The Romans clearly were a very convivial bunch of people, shame they did not have a newspaper or a book to read. I tend to believe that this was the point where they took conviviality a touch too far. I wonder if they tried this on the English when they crossed the channel – its cold up north.

If you carry on walking around the perimeter of these remarkable ruins you will come to the 11th Century Cathédrale Notre-Dame-de-Nazareth de Vaison. If you look closely  at the visible foundations and lower walls of the Cathedral you will see the reason as to why the Roman buildings are not as complete as they might have been as very obviously when the Romans left Provence the local people have used large quantities of pre-shaped Roman stone for the Cathedral.

Market day here in Vaison is on Tuesday morning as stipulated by order of Pope Clement VII in 1532 and Vaison market is one of the largest in the region with over 400 traders setting up stall and providing the most heady and delightful aromas of Provence. A great market but be warned it is always very busy and you may have to abandon your vehicle some distance from the centre of town and walk in. Get there early.

Yes, initially for us Vaison was merely a lunch stop but over the years we have visited the town for what it can offer the inquisitive visitor who likes his tourism supplied with a long lazy lunch with great historical views.

AVIGNON, PONT DU GARD AND OUR FIRST CHAMBRE D'HOTES

I t was back in  2002 that we first undertook the long drive of around 950 miles from the North of England down to the South of France. We had just picked up a brand new car and this was certainly a great test drive for it. Strictly speaking we were not staying in Avignon itself but in the small village of Pujaut to the north of Avignon and to the west of the river Rhone. The accomodation we had chosen was Les Bambous the home of Joel and Michele Rousseau and I believe they still offer rooms to the weary traveller as of now and I commend it to you.

We found Les Bambous in the small square adjacent to the village church - every village in France has at least one church. The large metal doors of the property facing onto the square did not overwhelm us with great expectation but they were opened by Michelle with such a warm welcome that it immediately became obvious that behind the cold exterior there was a hidden oasis of charm and good taste.

They are an artistic couple, photography and art, very personable although Joel is the quieter one, they quickly put us at ease. They offered us the choice of two rooms, one was a straightforward bedroom and en-suite bathroom and the other possibility was a small self-contained apartment that had its own cooking facilities. Although this one was to some degree a bit cave like having been built into the hillside and offering only a small amount of natural light, it did give us the option of buying our own food and cooking for ourselves if we desired. It also had access to the secluded garden above the main house which we liked.

We were kindly made an offer to share an evening meal with them if we wished as they were having a friend round for a meal and they thought it would be interesting for us to meet him. That was very kind and after having had a long day travelling we were very grateful for this offer although a little nervous about taking our first ever meal in a French home and meeting new people who spoke some English but would no doubt enjoy and be amused at hearing us trying out our French language skills.

After freshening up with a shower in the cave wet room and making a change of clothes we went back to the courtyard of this rambling property and we were met warmly with an aperitif before the arrival of their friend. There is no secret to their obvious success in running this small Bed and Breakfast here in Pujaut, just excellent unfussy warm genuine hospitality.

The courtyard is interesting in its decorative style in that it totally gives you the air of being in a shady secluded Moroccan courtyard coolly sheltered away from the blistering sun. The centrepiece in the stone floored courtyard is a large Moroccan tiled table with rounded ends, a large extended oval shape. It is very vibrant and fits in perfectly with the theme of the courtyard with the brightly coloured Moroccan lights situated above your head and small olive trees adding to the feeling of shade and peace. Their old friend duly arrives a little late and apologises and he is indeed as they promised an interesting man. It turns out he is a friend of theirs from way back and as we suspected from the way Les Bambous is themed they have all spent time together in Morocco and have an affectionate love of that country. Thiery runs a much larger Chambres d'Hote operation in Fez, Morocco and had flown in that day on some urgent business in Avignon. His lively conversation throughout the evening is engaging and his love and tales of travel that he clearly shares with Joel and Michele is fascinating. The tales of Fez and Morocco make you want to go and see it for yourself and he leaves a calling card with me and warmly offers us accommodation in Fez if we decide to make the journey.

Michele carries on the Moroccan theme into the preparation of the food for the evening and we share a chicken tagine with just a nod to France with a side dish of local vegetables made into a Ratatouille. Generous quantities of fine local wines make this a most convivial evening and the perfect start to our French experience of hospitality. Michele follows this excellent attention to her guests in the morning by presenting us with a beautiful simple breakfast of bread and croissants paired with home-made jams from local fruits and of course aromatic coffee. A feeling of well-being flows over us as it will so many times on our future French tours.

We are here in Avignon at the time of the famous summer festival and Joel and Michele have some commitment to that and have to go into Avignon a few times that week on Festival business. It is the very best of times to be visiting Avignon despite all the crowds and you are still able to park your car very easily right outside the city walls. Avignon in festival weeks is so vibrant and full of life and energy with street theatre everywhere around the central square as colourful enthusiastic players try to impress you enough to make it irresistible for you to want to see their full show in the evening. The scene around Avignon is packed full of colour and music with plays being partially acted out on the streets but in full costume. One such performance is obviously the Merchant of Venice and it is superbly done with the most vivid of costumes and certainly that must have helped fill the theatre in the evening

Just behind these actors and farther into the beautiful square there is a group of around 16 Peruvian musicians with guitars and pan pipes and they make the most gorgeous sound together. I am not exactly sure why they are here though or where they might be playing tonight but this is an eclectic festival, a bit like Edinburgh in Scotland but with sun.

This central square Place D'Horloge is vast but that is in itself dwarfed by the monumental 14th Century Palais de Papes. Avignon was the setting for the election of six popes in the 1300's and they were not going to slum it while they had to live here rather than in Rome during this turbulent period in history. It is an immense solid imposing residence that is surely more suited to repelling invaders than to spread the word of Christ but back then the Popes had many enemies and this towering Palace was indeed as much a fortress as a home.

Once inside the Palais you feel very small as you tour around the generously proportioned rooms but I found it is a slightly unrewarding visit for despite its magnificence there are no interior original fittings to speak of which is a shame. The Palace is relatively empty of interest inside except that is for the magnificent splendour of its architecture.

Avignon Cathedral Notre Dames des Doms can be reached with a short uphill stroll to the left of the vast

Palais. This Cathedral is quite an imposing structure in its own right but almost looks like a small afterthought added to the side of the Palais, almost totally dwarfed by the house of the Pope. The area around the Cathedral is a lovely spot to stroll or simply sit and contemplate the scene with excellent views gained from this higher vantage point. In some ways I would say this is a more enjoyable part of Avignon and a lot of visitors would probably by pass it and think it is just another part of the Palais des Papes. Through the gardens you can get right over to the other side of the old centre of town that brings into view Avignon Pont D'Avigon, Saint Benezete, the ancient half bridge that inspired the famous song. Views extend far back up the Rhone, taking in the islands produced by the split in the river laid out in front of you just upstream of Avignon. Just below you as you look across the river there is a tiny vineyard neatly set out and enclosed leading down to the riverside. The main vineyards producing refreshment for the benefit of the popes were of course upstream at Chateauneuf de Pape and that has maintained a reputation as an area of France synonymous with the very finest of fine wines.

Going back down the steps to the square we will meander for our lunch to La Fourchette restaurant on

Rue Racine near the Place de l'Horloge and I will describe that delightful establishment later in the book.

On this day, just outside the ancient walls and across the road that circulates around Avignon there is a large summer market and pleasure fair that ties in well with the atmosphere of the Festival. Here we find quite a few North African flavoured stalls including ones selling food and some others with their roots in places like Martinique and Guadeloupe. We bought some freshly prepared melon that would be enjoyed later over a glass of Lirac rosé wine at lunchtime tomorrow and also a set of wooden painted cats that you can rest along the edge of a bookcase. I have no idea why we did that!

Moving swiftly on.

Away from Avignon the Pont Du Gard is a destination somewhat like the Eiffel Tower in that you feel that it is a place you have to visit, it is one of the sights that come with the territory and you cannot go home without seeing it. It may be that you are not that bothered one way or the other but see it you must.

It has to be said that our decision to visit the bridge was something of an afterthought one day late in the afternoon, probably after a glass of wine.

Come on let's go.

We arrived at the parking and entrance area of the Pont du Gard quite late in the day, somewhere around 7 o'clock in the evening and all of the visitor facilities were closed and just a few cars were dotted across the large parking area. You could still access the walking route to the bridge and so we decided to stroll down the dusty path towards the Roman bridge. You pass on the way three incredible ancient olive trees, surely planted by the Roman gardener as landscaping when they built the bridge around two thousand years ago. These trees are twisted and knarled with trunks of enormous proportions. What they still do despite all their years in the ground is to produce olives and they look just as vigorous and vibrant as they would have done all those centuries ago.

You are not on this path very long before you get your first full view of this staggering feat of ancient engineering. The bridge was constructed in the first century AD to carry water the long distance from Uzes down to Nimes and this impressively arched three tiered structure across the Gardon river takes your breath away. There is nothing matter of fact about seeing this famous monument – it is unforgettable. The delightful thing about this from a tourist point of view is that you can actually walk over the full length of the structure and get a real sense of the astounding accomplishment this was. A bridge such as this would be a great achievement for modern engineers so you really do have to marvel at the skill and tenacity and endurance that these ancient builders showed – not forgetting the slave labour who surely must have earned their freedom.

By coming to the bridge so late in the day it gives it extra atmosphere and we feel it is quite special to view it at this hour and to be stepping on it in the glow of the setting sun in fading evening light. There is also the added bonus that there are so few tourists there at this time of the day and you have photo opportunities of the bridge being virtually deserted that could not be achieved earlier in the day. A truly marvellous sight. The only difficulty with coming at this time is that you do need to find your way back to your vehicle so take care to give yourself just enough daylight to do so.

This is simply not a tourist attraction to be blasé about but to have a sense of wonder and awe – simply to marvel at.

ROUSSILLON

J ustly famed as  one of the most beautiful villages in the Luberon, Roussillon is a place we have loved from the early days of our travels in Provence. Perched high like so many of the Luberon villages, Roussillon is surrounded by the most beautiful countryside and from the very top of the village it gives extensive panoramic views that are difficult to beat in any other village in the Luberon. As you drive up from the valley plain you lose sight of the village as you wind up the road around its base and then once again the beautiful sight of this lofty place comes into view – one of the best drives in the region. When you park up your car under the cliffs and start to take in how the village is constructed on the rocky outcrops, the village appears to be straddling more than one base of rock and looks quite precariously secured atop this summit. It is an impressive village and quite an achievement of a structure in times past.

The main feature that dominates Roussillon are the magnificent red cliffs and the red, yellow and brown shades of earth in the ochre quarries. It is a stunning sight. The large amounts of ochre deposits around Roussillon are the largest to be found in the world. The whole setting of Roussillon is just magical as you see interspersed around the village setting lush pine trees that contrast vibrantly with the ochre and the stunning clear blue Provencal skies. It is an area of incredible natural light and this of course has attracted a succession of artists to the village. Our friend Francoise is one of the modern resident artists and for us it has been a pleasure to be able to visit her in the studio where for many years she has worked here in Roussillon, she is a very talented and successful artist in this village. Do make sure that you pay her studio a visit located at the beginning of the climb to the top of the village. The last time we visited Francoise I had to explain that her beautiful paintings were at the moment just a little outside my price range but she kindly gave us a signed print and this takes pride of place in our home after we had it framed. It is a lovely reminder of the colours of Roussillon and happy times.

 Roussillon is an exceptionally atmospheric village to stroll around and the maze of narrow streets are a joy to walk and can be a welcome source of shade on a hot Provencal day. The houses are composed of many different shades of ochre tints and these colours are perfectly set off by the brightly painted shutters framing the windows. Roussillon has quite a number of reliable cafes and restaurants particularly to be found as you make your way up towards the 11th Century chapel Eglise Saint Michel church and the summit. This is a small intimate church and is very cool inside but fairly simply adorned. This is a good place to rest for a while as you make your way to the top of the village and take in the stunning views.

Just around the corner and higher up from the church is a shop that sells pottery and ochre pigments. As I write this now I can see in the room the large olive green jug that we bought from there many years ago and it is a beautiful piece that reminds us of our visit and is always on display. It took a bit of carrying back to the car in the baking heat. We also made a big mistake by buying some ochre pigments that we felt sure would make our kitchen walls back home both unique and beautiful.

They most certainly made them unique.

The problem was in those pre 'Google and You Tube knows everything' days was that we had neglected to find out how to use them correctly. We had assumed that it was a simple matter of mixing with white paint and off you go. Apparently not. The colour of our kitchen walls of our cottage turned into a bizarre mix of a brown, purple and red sludge like mess of a finish. It had taken some time and effort to achieve this awful result so we thought that maybe it would settle down and the resulting hues would grow on us. It was clear after we had received sufficient visitors to cast their judgement over this garish fiasco that it was purely and simply dreadful and we had to repaint the entire kitchen, our dream of a Roussillon ochre inspired kitchen shattered.

This shop is close to the top of the village and when reaching the summit you find the most amazing view of what appears to be the entire Luberon and beyond. A breath taking place to sit and wonder for a time until the burning sun takes its toll on our fair skins.

Roussillon is a must see village and along with our quieter favourite Bonnieux, a village that can be seen across the valley plain, it is a place we return to as often as we possibly can.

ISLE SUR LA SORGUE

Isle sur la Sorge is a name synonymous with the very best of French markets, particularly antique or flea markets. It is certainly a town worth visiting in its own right as it has many pleasing antique shops and other independent shops as well as an extensive choice of restaurants around the River Sorgue and leading off into the narrow winding streets of the town.

On one of our first visits to the Sunday market we came across the travel writer and broadcaster Anne Gregg who was undoubtedly there because she loved France but specifically was researching for her forthcoming book on French markets and Isle sur la Sorgue is certainly at the forefront of those. She produced a wonderfully informative book called 'Tarragon and Truffles' shortly afterwards but sadly died in that same year of its publication. It is one of my favourite travel books and the most used and thumbed through of books and if you have any interest in the markets of France then I do urge you to obtain a copy. It might now be over a decade old but it is always the first book in my suitcase when we are travelling to France.

Although there is a market in Isle sur la Sorgue on Saturday and Monday it is the market on Sunday that is the one you will find is the most interesting market to visit. The Sunday market also has alongside the antiques and bric a brac stalls the full range of food specialities produced in the region and plenty of other artisans and interesting stalls. These spread out right into the town down the narrow streets that lead you into the square. Be aware that the Sunday market is extremely popular and busy and definitely a most sensible idea is to arrive in the town early. I have always found that you can get a parking space albeit you may have to be prepared to walk about 500 yards or so to the market itself. The streets and the riverside are thronged with people when you are browsing around and you do need to be patient with your fellow man and go with the flow, literally and metaphorically.

I do recall on one occasion we had the attentions of the local 10 year old Mafia. We parked our car eventually down a side road that led to a dusty track with some open space next to a small sports ground. A small space was available to squeeze the car into. As we walked away towards the market we had to pass three young local boys with their equally young female assistant who were pleased to let us know that for a small fee our car would still be there in its original condition on our return. As I could tell it was there only source of income and feeling sure that the condition of the car might be somewhat different if I ignored their business proposition I handed over my cash. True to their word the car was fine but the market enterprise starts early so be warned.

The antique and bric a brac stalls are the finest and most interesting I have seen outside of Paris and they are not short on quality as well as offering the enthusiast the opportunity to buy endless amounts of what we seem to refer to these days as pre-loved furniture and interior design items for the home. It is an interior designers dream. If you had a large van with you it does not need much imagination to realise that you could easily transform your home into true authentic French shabby chic on a single visit.

On our very first Sunday market we found and continued to return many times to a man who sells fish, well specifically salmon and he comes from a village close to Avignon. It is a small but perfectly formed food stall where you have to be very patient and just enjoy watching this craftsman, an artist at work. A man that is so proud of his produce that his enthusiasm oozes from his every pore and his gentle words reflect his pride as he describes the produce that he is so delicately preparing for your pleasure. He attracts a crowd of devoted regulars and I am happy to be one of them if you can count a visit to him every one or two years as being a regular customer. He also sells cured ham produced in the style of Serrano ham and gently shaves into impossibly thin slices with his very sharp long knife. It is the salmon though that is his real 'baby' and you have to wait while he gently prepares it and lovingly wraps the fish as if for a cadeaux to take to your loved one as a perfect present. You wait as he explains its provenance, its delicate taste and texture and offers advice as to how you might enjoy it to the full. It is an extraordinary level of customer service and yes you can be there for quite a long time but every word he says about his exquisite product will become apparent as being totally true when you eat it that evening with a crisp chilled local rosé wine.

There are many artisan cheese producers having stalls on this market with tempting displays and other small scale producers that may only be offering a single cheese prepared in their own kitchen back at the farm or smallholding. These cheeses are superb but be careful when you are buying. I always find that no matter how much I ask for that you seem to end up with twice that quantity and your expected five Euro purchase can become much more. I learnt that the hard way the first time I bought and ended up with so much cheese that we took some home but it was a superb hard cheese and I have to say a pleasure to enjoy again once back in England.

Lunch is easy to find here but not easy to choose – there is so much choice – from the many well priced restaurants lining the duck filled gentle river with its old waterwheel or ones to be found winding through the town or with all the delicious street food on offer. Our favourite stall is the Chinese food vendor by the river who has been there all the years we have been going to Isle sur la Sorgue. His food is delicious and authentic and to be enjoyed in the shade on the island that bisects the river or to take home for a lazy lunch well away from the crowds.

Isle sur la Sorgue is special and once you have

been here for the market then do make sure that you visit again on a non-market day and then in the quiet of the town discover many more interesting shops that were totally obscured from view on your market day visit.

The Sunday morning market at nearby Coustellet is a good alternative if you do not fancy coping with the crowds at Isle sur la Sorgue and once again here on this market you are spoilt for choice with all the local produce, particularly melons, peaches and other fruits. On our last visit here we bought some small sweet tomatoes of various different colours and they were superb that evening with our home made garlic bread that we constructed from bread bought from a baker on his aromatic stall that had so many varieties we wondered at what time of the night he and his team must have begun to bake it all. The garlic we sourced later in Sault higher up the valley on our essential quest for the lavender fields. Alongside the tomatoes and bread we bought some fabulous juicy local melon – the knowledgeable producer who as always was so proud and enthusiastic about his produce even asked me at what time of day we would be eating it. I have to say that question was a little puzzling to me as I am just used to buying melon shrink wrapped with a sell by date on it. He explained that he just wanted to ensure that he sold me a melon that would be just at the point of perfection when we sliced into it to enjoy. Talk about attention to detail. All of this produce from the markets gave us a delightful supper under the cool veranda back at the cottage that was our home on this trip.

TAILLADES

L es Taillades is a small medieval village in the Luberon, it is an ancient village constructed in stone and the evidence  of its importance as a quarrying centre has endured down to today. At the top of the village is to be found the historical centre and its perched church near the old stone quarries. Below, is the Canal of Carpentras and its superb 19th Century Moulin Saint Pierre. The imposing outline of the water-wheel of the Moulin Saint Pierre is reflected in the old canal and alongside the waterway there are splendid one hundred-year-old plane trees.

There are a wide variety of plants and flowers to appreciate and these subtle scents permeate the village and surroundings. As you can in many parts of Provence, enjoy the relaxing song of the cicadas, at first seemingly boring deep into your head to make it explode but then settling to a soothing hum and rhythm of calm.

It is a bucolic place - We did not stay here.

The address on the confirmatory email was Les Taillades but actually our gite was to be found just outside the village. Our initial severe disappointment as we drove through the small industrial complex and eventually coming to a stone wall containing a small green door and post box was about to dissipate. This was indeed our home for the week - on an industrial complex. Typical of the French planners to allow such a monstrosity to be built in the middle of such beauty but as we were greeted at the door by our lady host and shown behind the wall we then found the most beautiful oasis of calm. This was a charming Provencal villa with extensive tree lined grounds and a large warm pool.

Our apartment was separate to the main large house that is home to our host Suzanne. It was clean, well presented and equipped and the terrace gave no hint or sight of the industrial complex it backed onto but rather a very beautiful Provencal garden view with the Alpilles mountain range as a stunning backdrop.

Madam came round to the apartment to see if we were settled in and pleased with our accommodation and invited us to join her for supper which we gladly accepted. Gladly that is until she uttered those dreaded words:

'I have a speciality in the fridge for my English guests to enjoy'.

And we all know what that means.

We were greeted enthusiastically in the large farmhouse kitchen by Suzanne and she warmly introduced a lady friend who was also going to stay for supper.

Pleasantries over we all sat down at the long antique wooden farmhouse table and after pouring a glass of wine for us Suzanne brought out her 'special starter'.

Yes, of course it was Fois Gras.

I have managed to eat Fois Gras before if pushed hard enough but it is still one of my worst nightmares to be given this in a meal although I can usually eat just about anything now after all our travels in France with many meals being anything but 'a la carte'.

Fois Gras is still for me a bridge too far.

This portion was a particularly awful example of this peculiarly French delicacy. Sat before me was a hideous warm slab of prepared seared liver on a thick piece of garlic toast - seemingly taunting me from the plate. My eating of it started off OK but I could see immediately that this would be a challenge to say the least. This slice of some poor ducks innards was slowly but surely decomposing before my eyes. The spongy slimy texture was seemingly melting and fine ribbons of blood started oozing out of every pore as it started to spread over the plate. The one saving grace of the presentation and my only way out of this was that like a melting ice cream it was gradually reaching a texture that I could sweep beneath some salad leaves and eventually give an impression to my host that I had thoroughly enjoyed this special treat and hoping that she did not notice that most of it was in fact still somewhere on my plate. It was without doubt or competition the very worse food experience I ever had in France. The rest of the meal I recall feeling was very good, a spicy Senegalese Chicken Yassa but I can't exactly remember anything about it now, I can only remember the biology lesson that was the first course.

SUZETTE

If you were going to ask me which single place in the whole of Provence would I without fail have to visit on every trip that I may make to the region then my answer would be the small and lovely hilltop village of Suzette. It is by far the tiniest place I have written about but what it lacks in size it more than makes up for in beauty and location. Yes, this is my favourite location to be standing and admiring in all of Provence.

You will find it in the heart of the Dentelles de Montmirail on the eastern side. Suzette is a tiny village clinging to a rocky outcrop at an altitude of more than 400 metres and you will reach it by taking the road from Malaucene or Beames de Venise, both of these are beautiful spectacular drives. The village has few houses and inhabitants, one small restaurant and a wine producer that sells wine, honey and other local products. These although welcome are not the reason I love this place. It is the views.

Looking back from the village plateau over the rows of grape vines you get the most stunning panorama of the Dentelles de Montmirail and yes, as the name suggests the jagged formation does resemble crooked teeth. For me this is one of the finest views in France, a truly spectacular sight that on a hot sunny day with cloudless skies is a photographer's dream opportunity. I have met many an English speaking tourist when arriving into Suzette and the reaction from them is always the same – 'Have you seen THAT.'

The route back to Beames will of course reward you with magnificent views as you follow alongside the Dentilles and in the village of Beames you will find the famous sweet wine of the area. Going to Malaucene the road winds down the hillside more steeply but you get more staggering panoramic views of the white peak of Mont Ventoux in the distance. My favourite route is by taking the third way out of Suzette down a narrow road through the delightful vineyards that surround the village and find my way down to Le Barroux.

There you need to look out for the olive groves and if you feel able then have the confidence to drive

up one of the long wind-
ing driveways through the
groves and have a tasting,
buying some for home.
You will not regret being
able to savour this dark
green nectar in the winter
back home. I do then put

this area around Suzette as my unmissable destination
on tour in Provence.

CHATEAU VAL JOANIS

My plan is to write later as one separate subject about our exploits in wine touring, visiting vineyards and producers and also the experiences on some organized wine tours as a group and with friends.

I cannot however write about Provence and our times there without including the Chateau Val Joanis located near to Pertuis in my writings as it has played such an important part in our travels and times in this beautiful region.

Sometime back in the mid 1990's the English chef and bon viveur Keith Floyd filmed a series about the wine regions of France and on the Provencal leg of the trip he filmed at Chateau Val Joanis.

Floyd was not a chef that ever inspired me to cook anything specific from his programmes or writings but what he did achieve because of his enthusiasm was to make me want to look at French food and wines more seriously and also his love of France as a country was infectious. To many he was perhaps more an entertainer than a chef but his extraordinary personality and love of food and wine did more than most to move British cooking and inspire the chefs that followed into a higher level and quality than had been the case with British food before him. His appearance at Chateau Val Joanis was a case in point of entertainment taking over from a serious consideration of the wine but in the end the same result was achieved – I just had to go there.

Along with his Master of Wine sidekick Jonathan Pedley who certainly was 'kicked' by Floyd along the way on this wine crawl (sorry tour) around France they tasted the superb range of wines on offer at Val Joanis. Unfortunately and I suspect deliberately simply for dramatic effect they tasted these wines outside the chateau in the blazing summer sun with not a hint of shade. The red wines must have been tasted at least around 10 degrees above the recommended temperature and it was obviously so hot that they were clearly on the verge of collapse. Combining the searing heat with the wine consumption they seemed to be suffering from dehydration. All this made brilliant TV but certainly was not ideal for sampling the wines but I never forgot it so Val Joanis got some future sales from me and I have no doubt from many others who saw this classic piece of filming.

We visited Val Joanis quite a number of times when travelling in this region and one wine – Red Cuvee Les Griottes – has become our house wine if you like, the one bottle we always serve to special friends. It is gorgeous, a blend of Syrah and Grenache and barrel aged for 10 months. It is a fairly strong wine, rich in red fruits and slightly smoky from the oak aging. Our friends along with us view this as our very favourite wine brought back from France over the years. Don't stop there though if you visit this vineyard as they have splendid white and rosé wines alongside other red wines that compliment Les Griottes in the range.

One visit to Val Joanis stands out in the memory. It is this one from July 2010 and these are my recollections of it written at the time:

Today our destination was to be Chateau Val Joanis vineyard near Pertuis in the Southern Luberon. We have been here several times before and their wines are a firm favourite not just of ours but our friends at home who always await our return expectantly with wine glass in hand, finding our car boot fully loaded.

On arriving at Val Joanis we first of all strolled around the magnificent gardens and on this visit they are even finer now than when we last came two years previously. The talented gardeners have produced a really beautiful mix of planting interspersing fruits and vegetables within the main areas of flowers, trees and shrubs. The extensive lavender planting is superb and fragrant as is the shrub lined arbor as you head through to be presented with even more vineyard views in the countryside beyond. They leave fruit and vegetables out in crates for you to freely take and enjoy.

The long driveway winding its way into the domain gives a panoramic view of the vineyards and olive groves – it is very beautiful. You get an idea of the type of 'terroir' found at Val Joanis and in this region as we ease the car over the pebbly rocky drive and it is this terroir that gives the wines of Val Joanis their distinctive aroma and flavour. (By the way, the drive of today is not as rocky and there is no need to bring a 4 by 4 vehicle to reach the domain.)

In the tasting room some other fellow wine lovers had arrived before us so to enjoy a tasting we joined on with a couple of English men who were just starting out on their wine exploration and we were pleasantly and knowledgably guided through an extensive selection by a charming German girl who spoke excellent French and English (and German).

When we had got around halfway through the wines on offer she was asked just how she came to be here in Provence - she was heartfelt as she replied that:

'She came here for love but love went away and then she found the love of the vines'.

That to us sounded definitely more in tune with the sentiments of a French girl really and there was not a dry eye between us hardened Brits – but we rallied with true British stiff upper lip spirit as we focused once again on the task in hand seeing that she had more wines on her wooden barrel for us to taste.

And what a tasting she gave us – she did not stint on that, she was so generous. Between us we tasted at least eight or nine wines including an extremely rare

2003 Cuvee Les Griottes Red that was now only available to purchase in small 50cl bottles. This was very generous indeed and for us to take back to England and the long cold winter nights we settled on a case of 2006 Les Griottes and also a case of its companion white. Both of these came in wooden boxes and one of these still gives faithful service as a container for fresh bread in our kitchen, the liquid contents long ago very happily consumed. Why buy wine any other way? What a joy to find such fabulous wines in a beautiful setting and such friendly and generous hospitality.

Yes, Floyd may not have savoured the best possible expression of the wines in his meltdown tasting here at the Chateau but he did point me in the direction of a wine that has given a lot of pleasure to myself and many friends – a fine legacy.

ESCAPE IN THE LUBERON

N ot often, in fact only really this once, have things gone badly wrong in our quest for independent travel in France. I am obsessively careful in choosing accommodation and travel – obsessively careful. I love to take time over a long English winter to narrow down our choices and check reviews and of course use my gut feelings about a Bed and Breakfast, hotel or a self-catering stay. I have to say that this research nearly always pays off and there are no unpleasant surprises when we arrive tired after a long journey at some tranquil haven of peace and hospitality. This time in the rural countryside close to Menerbes it was anything but and turned into quite a dramatic escape from the gite from hell.

During my browsing of possibilities during the winter I came across the Slow Travel website, not one that I had looked at before. On this website there was a blog with photos about a self-catering gite located on a vineyard set below the village of Menerbes well away from the main road heading towards Bonnieux. This blog was written by a Canadian couple who claimed to have spent two weeks at this gite and it all sounded quite idyllic. Along with their children they had enjoyed the produce of the farm and helped out on the vineyard, extolling the virtues of this quiet healthy travel experience. It was a most convincing article and unfortunately for me my usual ability of reading between the lines of articles like this sadly deserted me. What could be better than this for us with our love of wine and local produce than to stay surrounded by vines and be able to interact with an enthusiastic wine growing family?

Anything as it turned out would have been better.

It had been a long journey down from Burgundy

from our overnight stay but as it turned out we had fortunately arrived quite early in Vaison La Romain for lunch before heading on to Menerbes. Vaison is a place that always puts you in good humour for your visit to Provence and after an enjoyable lunch in the old town we were ready for the short hop to Menerbes and our rural home for the next week. We arrived below the village about 3pm at the poorly maintained track leading from the main road. There were no signs but from the directions contained in the email this appeared to be the correct place. The dusty rutted track was seemingly endless as we drove through some barren scrubland dotted with some old untended olive trees and half expecting a wild boar to run out in front of the car. It was bakingly hot and clouds of dust were rising behind the car no matter how slowly I drove. The track was rutted and gave the impression that it would be quite impassable in winter without a 4 by 4 or tractor to get you through. Finally we saw the farmhouse with a man we assumed must be the vigneron owner working out in front of it tending to some vines that came in slightly untidy rows right up to the house. He motioned to us to pass by the house and head to the rear of the property which we did without stopping having got the impression that he was a man of few words. When you go to most accommodations other than hotels in France and particularly staying away from the larger towns it is generally the lady of the house that handles the practicalities of your stay. The man has man's work and for a Frenchman that does not include what he would perceive as domestic duties. His place is set in the land tending the soil and its produce or in most cases of older Frenchmen occupying a café bar table on a terrace in the village square. I generalise but you get the picture.

Just as we pass by the rear corner of the ancient stone mas we encounter a merry band of itinerant farm labourers, merry in the best imbibing of cheap wine sense. To a man and woman they wave us around to the other side of the property but seemingly finding the whole thing very amusing. This turns out to be not because of some alcoholic stupor but simply that the joke truly was on us.

As we wheel round to the other side I recognise from the Slow Travel blog photos the gite that we had booked with such high hopes back in the winter. It was a poor first impression – can't believe I understated it like that. On the veranda, constructed a bit like you see on movies and documentaries about the American wild west, you know the sort of place you would tether your horse, were some grim looking towels and cloths. I assume they had been washed but I am not sure what they had been washed in. No matter, we still naively had high expectations.

Those expectations were shattered the moment we opened the door. There was to be no welcoming basket of wine and foodie goodies here. It was apparent that the place had not been prepared at all. In the living space was some bizarre huge piece of dark late 19th century French furniture that surely must have come from a large chateau, full of crockery, pans and anything else that was not required to be on view. Enormous and hideous piece it was but not only that it was filthy with the top part showing signs of never having been cleaned from new. The local spiders had clearly brought up many generations of families there.

Into the kitchen and the old fridge was still either expecting its previous occupants to return or they were growing some bacterial cultures for research purposes. The sink was full of uncleaned pans.

What to do? For some reason that to this day I still cannot comprehend how, we decided to see if it really was not as bad as it seemed. Niamh set about cleaning the kitchen, especially the fridge. I unloaded the boot of the car and said I would travel into Menerbes and get some basic provisions. Our optimism here has absolutely no basis in the reality around us but perhaps because we had developed a basic trust in people we rented from in France we were reluctant to admit that what we saw around us was really quite disgusting.

So I headed off back along that dusty track into Menerbes leaving Niamh to try to turn the gite into a liveable place to stay. How I still regret that. In Menerbes I found that curiously French store that seems to be in every village, one that has everything you could possibly need housed in a very small space. Fresh vegetables, meat, fish, cheese, bread, canned everything and of course even matches for the fire and shampoo for your hair. In England and I am sure in the US we have vast supermarkets filled for aisle after aisle with everything our hearts could desire purporting to be saying that this is just what we need. Here though in this little shop run by a friendly lady is everything certainly I and most people could possibly need. We are certainly fooled and obsessed with consumerism back home. It did not take me long to gather my needs and get back to the car hurrying back to the gite.

Down the track the clouds of dust were massive as I sped back to see how Niamh was getting on. Once inside I could see that she was still in the kitchen, in fact still with the fridge door open.

Niamh's head peered out from the fridge and she said 'Just look at this' and showed me the bedroom and the situation we were in got even worse. The pillows were uncovered and had the clear brown outline of the heads of many previous users. This was nothing like the gushing review the Slow Travel blog had described and I cannot conceive that anyone could have stayed in such conditions and given such a glowing review. Not unless they were deficient in several of their senses. I certainly wished my senses were less highly tuned at that moment.

This situation was hopeless.

We took one look at each other and I exclaimed:

'Everything back in the car – NOW'

Fortunately we had unpacked very little inside the gite and soon we gathered our possessions up and pretty much threw them in to the car. I scribbled a note in French on a scrap of paper stating to the owner just how disgusting the place was. We were lucky that madam had not come round to see us as yet for final payment and we had only committed a small deposit to her.

Leaving only a trail of dust as we sped off back around the rear of the large farmhouse, past the smirking transient vineyard labourers and the bemused owner who was still tending his garden we headed off down the long winding dusty drive that would take us back to the main road.

About half way down the drive I slammed on the brakes.

My camera! I have left it back in the gite. My camera was not an inexpensive one as I love my photography but there was absolutely no way I could go back to the gite. I bolted out from the car and looking back I could see a crowd of people in front of the farmhouse, pointing and staring accusingly through the cloud of dust down the track at us. I opened the car boot and everything was in a complete tangled mess and I frantically pulled things aside and tried to search through this heap of stuff we had created by simply throwing everything back in the car. Eventually and thankfully, there was my camera, I had put the camera in with everything else. Quickly rearranging the boot so that it would close I got back into the driver's seat and away we went again, checking that no pickup trucks were following us.

Paranoia had certainly set in and I desired to put as much distance as possible between this awful place containing possibly angry owners and our car, so by taking a back roads route we reached the D900 and Coustellet and then on by the D901 towards L'Isle sur la Sorgue and freedom. That was just the most awful welcome to our time in Provence and I have to admit that the stress levels were high but we now quickly had to refocus because what we did not have at this moment in time was somewhere to stay and it was starting to get late in the day.

Driving on but all the while looking out for any potential places to stay we headed past L'Isle sur la Sorgue and towards Pernes les Fontaines. There was nothing so far that had any promise as somewhere to stay other than for us trying to find a hotel temporarily just for the night. Most gites or Bed and Breakfasts in the area had 'complete' signs on the entrance. We really wanted to find somewhere for us to be able to self-cater for the week and unpack and get settled but we were tired and frustrated and losing hope. In these ignorant days before Trip Advisor and instant 'finds' on your iPhone all you could do was to drive around and seek something out but this process wasn't doing much for our state of mind at all.

On the road to Pernes we saw a sign for a complex of gites.

I think it said something like:

'Paradise Gites await you at the end of the drive' or something similar.

We drove down the long straight plane tree lined drive and sure enough at the end there was a vision of Paradise. This was a conversion of a large old stone mas and it's outbuildings into gites and chamber d'hotes accommodation. Children were playing in the beautiful pool with some of the parents sat in the chairs around this pool sipping on their first rosé wine of the evening. Truly this is our place to be, our refuge from the appalling day we have had, we belong HERE. I get out and can hear voices inside the mas through open double doors. I step into the most delightful farmhouse kitchen, with a long antique farmhouse table at its centre where the most contented and happy group of people were preparing the evening meal. Laid out on the table was fresh produce from the market and beautiful aromas coming from cooking on the large oven range. All in the kitchen were cooking and preparing in the best way possible, wine glass in hand or by their side. I really do belong here. I must unfortunately though look like an intruder from another planet, quite bedraggled and certainly stressed and my appearance at the door does stop them in their tracks and food preparation ceases as they all turn to gaze at the temerity of my intrusion.

I manage to blurt out in broken French that we are looking for a gite or chambres d'hotes for the week and do they please, please have anything available. They do not and I am crushed, this as the evening light was fading had to be our last hope. Paradise was full and the occupants of Paradise were not to be honest overly interested in this straggler from the north of England and I could only turn away and retreat. It was clear that I was not one of them, at least not until I came back after having a shower and attired myself in fresh clean clothes, preferably designer ones. I bet they had a gite but I think they might have been worried about the stains I might leave on some fresh, crisp bed sheets. Maybe they knew about where we had escaped from and did not want their pillowcases soiled. At least we had a glimpse of what life could be like here in Provence but we were sent packing. A cleaner fresher version of us could have made this home, I could have cooked for them, they would have liked that, but it was not to be.

Where do we go from here - where indeed? Then

I remembered that we were not that far now from the small village of Mazan located at the foot of the route that takes you over to Sault. We had stayed in Mazan in a good sized apartment owned by an English lady named Adrianne a couple of years earlier and that also had been a total disaster of a week for very different reasons but through no fault of Adrianne or indeed Provence. That is another story that I may tell if I can summon up the courage.

I did not have her telephone number but we could be there in around half an hour. The obvious and in my mind insurmountable problem was that I knew that she only had one apartment and it was an extremely good one so the chances of it being un-occupied were very slim but we had no other options. We had also strayed in to a part of Provence that was quite rural and it was now going dark so our options were few, other than maybe heading back towards Avignon and finding a hotel. So off to find Adrienne was the plan, the final last hope.

Mazan is a strange place. I mean that in the good sense of the word. It is to all intents a walled village but that is not actually obvious when you first see it. The 'walls' are made up of ancient houses all joined together to make up a 'wall' the entire way around the village. You enter into the village through small passageways, gates if you will and there really is nothing inside but more stone houses and a church that has a bell tower that strikes on the hour day and night. I remember it well. As far as I could establish there are no shops inside the 'walls' just one or two outside on the perimeter and a pizza restaurant. It does oddly for this type of village boast a high end hotel restaurant Chateau de Mazan which does look at this moment like a Paradise alternative I can tell you.

Adrianne's house is just inside the walls close to a small bridge on the 'ring road' of Mazan. There is just about room to take a car in to the narrow street but it is easier to park outside the walls of Mazan. The old stone house was originally a boulongerie but although you can still see a faded painted sign on the outside walls this must have last been operating as such quite some time ago. The entrance hall in to the house is fairly dark but it soon opens up into a lovingly restored old French property. Adrianne, after some determined bell ringing and knocking on the door is in residence and opens the door to us. We are desperate and I am sure she can see that. She is first of all though pleased to see us and she remembered us clearly from our previous visit two years ago. Our hopes now rest on her rental property being unoccu-pied but she does as anticipated have clients already settled in the apartment. This day goes from bad to worse and I sense we must head back to Avignon and find a hotel but that means we will lose time on our stay in Provence being unable to find a place to settle and enjoy. Adrianne then says that she does have a newly renovated apartment but it is not yet completely finished but we are welcome to look at it and if we are content with the amount of renovation already completed we are welcome to stay there. We would have stayed in a tent in the garden.

The apartment is absolutely fine, perhaps just short of the floor coverings being finalised and one or two 'snagging' jobs for the French artisan to complete but we are more than content to take this apartment for the week. Adrianne lets it out to us at a gener-ous rate and we slump into the apartment, utterly ex-hausted both physically and mentally from a day that started so promisingly in Burgundy but turned into a nightmare farce that we had the starring role in.

Adrianne makes everything better that week and it becomes one of our very best times in Provence. The weather is superb the entire week and we tour this picturesque area of rural quiet Provence eating and drinking our way through long lunches and cooking the regions fresh produce in the evening or sitting in the sheltered garden by the pool.

Adrianne invites us to her table during the week and we meet our fellow guests and Adrianne's friends. One of these is a very talented artist named Francoise Valenti who has a studio in Roussillon village. Francoise is very successful in her art career and sells much of her work to Americans. A well-travelled, very interesting and lovely person to have met and we have been able to visit her again at her studio in the years following but we are now very much overdue in saying hello to her again. We will be back to Provence soon Francoise.

Our week in Provence was saved by Adrianne's kindness. The experience taught me to be even more cautious when deciding where to stay in France and I became fastidiously so - almost to the point of paranoia.

Never again did we come even close to suffering the indignity of this day and all of our future stays in France turned out to be excellent and rewarding. That is travel though, it is all about experiences and some may not be what you expected but most will be memorable for good or bad. What a day but ultimately it became a great week.

AIX EN PROVENCE - IN SEARCH OF CÉZANNE

I f you were to
question me forcefully and
make me confess then I
would probably say that if
you exclude food and wine
then my most favourite facet of the Culture and Art of
France would have to be the paintings of the Impressionists.

Provence and its landscape are synonymous primarily with Paul Cézanne if you discount the issue with Van Goghs ear that is. Paul Cézanne was born and later died in Aix en Provence and although a proportion of his output was carried out in Paris it is his work in Provence and particularly in Aix that probably are more well-known and appeal to people as quintessential Cézanne. I have always since taking an interest in Impressionism admired and enjoyed his work. I have seen many of his and the other Impressionists art works in Museums in Paris especially at the Musee D'Orsay and it is a thrill to see such great art at close quarters. I have not however visited Aix, so it is time to put that right.

Cézanne lived much of his life in Provence and for some of that time he had the difficult task of hiding from his father the fact that he had a son, Paul, by his mistress Hortense. His father to a degree supported Cézanne in his chosen career by means of an allowance which would be lost to him if he was discovered to be living contrary to his father's standards.

This delicate situation was ultimately resolved and he gained a studio at the family home Bastide du Jas de Bouffan in Aix. His complex relationship with Hortense was by the start of the 20th Century very strained and he was now in the last decade of his life. Cézanne needed peace and somewhere to be alone with his painting so he built an isolated studio high up above the town of Aix on the Chemin des Lauves, now known at the Atelier Paul Cézanne and open to the general public. We should visit so we set of towards Aix, a place that would be a new experience but a town I had high expectations of in view of its illustrious son.

On arriving in Aix we first of all decided to walk

down the Cours Mirabeau and browse the shops and restaurants lining both sides. This is of course the main street in Aix and although not as famous as the Champs Elysees in Paris is the thoroughfare that you most closely associate with Aix and it tries to be just as trendy as Paris. It is a beautiful street with many fountains along the way and lined with old plane trees giving shade in front of the shops, cafes and restaurants. No question though it can be a tourist trap and prices on the terraces of the cafes can be high but what a spot for people watching. This is the place to see and be seen in Aix en Provence.

We deviated our way off the Cours Mirabeau through narrow streets and passageways to reach the Place Richelme where there is a local produce food market held every day of the week. This small, tightly packed square encapsulates every sight, sound and more importantly smell of your mental image of a market in Provence. Fresh bread, vast range of cheeses, meats, cold air dried saucisson of course, mushrooms, fruits of the region and some hot food stalls especially the tempting chicken rotisserie with the potatoes being sautéed in the cooking juices. Interspersed between are flower stalls and along with the incredible smells from the olive sellers they turn the square into a glorious assault on the senses.

Stopping for a coffee at Bar de l'Horloge at the end of the market we then retraced our steps back up the length of the Cours Mirabeau to the underground car park and made our way up to Atelier Paul Cézanne, not too far from the centre of Aix. The area is un-promising, very 1970's apartments and the studio is quite difficult to find. I park the car in amongst the apartments and walk through to find the studio of Cézanne. I have the feeling that the area was a lit-tle different back in the time Cézanne had this studio built, peace and tranquillity would be a little bit harder for him to find today.

The studio of Cézanne though does give out the impression of an oasis of calm and the views he would have enjoyed around the area and down the hill to-wards the centre of Aix would in his day have been quite beautiful. The house has the ubiquitous French shutters that you would expect to see in the South, painted in that faded matt red/brown that seemed to be beloved of the impressionists. You can see the same colour on shutters and doors in the village of Giverny, famous as the home of Monet in the last decades of his life. Immediately inside the house you collect your ticket and to be honest find that the first impression (sorry) is not very promising. There is little to catch your attention that may in some way relate to Cézanne's time here but the scene changes dramatically for the better as you ascend the stairs up to his studio. As soon as you step inside this magical space you are transported back in time, over a hundred years, to what appears to be a studio that is still being used to create great art. As you stand in the centre you imagine looking over your shoulder towards the door and seeing Cézanne walking briskly through, ready for a day of creation. One of the most atmospheric rooms I have been in.

You could argue you are let down to a degree in that there is nothing here that Cézanne actually created, there are no finished works as of course these almost priceless objects are now in museums or private collections. That is though what makes this room special.

You have to imagine.

You have to look at the objects, the high artist steps, the large easel, the tables and drawers seemingly left as they were when he last left the room, still ready for use. Other props Cézanne used such as the pottery, baskets and fruit. There is the wood and canvas deckchair with footrest. You see the selection of books neatly resting on the bookcase. The crucifix placed high on the wall, reflecting Cézanne's conversion to Catholicism quite late in his life. The skulls that Cézanne painted in his last works as he contemplated his mortality knowing that he was coming to the end of his life here in Aix. You feel that Cézanne, if he walked in would not notice the many admirers who have visited his studio today and would simply set up his easel and start to paint, calm and happy in his own space. Like many other places in France I appreciate being able to let my imagination wander and fill the space from my mind's eye. This is how I like my history and the Atelier Paul Cézanne is a joy.

We take our leave and go outside, past the climbing plants and stone plant troughs, past the pretty metal table and chairs and back into modernity and our car. Where to next in our search for Cézanne? Inevitably it has to be a view of Montagne Sainte Victoire and we head out of Aix on the A8 AutoRoute.

The mountain range of St Victoire is impressive and is a considerable length of formidable rock. If you can spend a little time here then what you do appreciate about this range is that the thing that most impressed and inspired Cézanne was obviously the play of light on the ridged exterior of the mountain.

That is still the same, unaffected by climate change. As with most outdoor artists Cézanne loved the effect of changing light and you certainly are aware of that spectacle when casting your eyes on this famous mountain.

It would have been ideal for us to have gone to the fishing village of L'Estaque, another spot that was synonymous with Paul Cézanne. We decided on a compromise. Instead we headed to the coast and the village of Cassis. We also wanted to call at the village of Bandol and Domaine Tempier and purchase some of their heady Bandol red wine.

I am not sure how familiar Cézanne was with the wines of Bandol but at Cassis port we were very aware of the spectacular light that Cézanne would have treasured when creating his works of art in this region. He surely must have enjoyed the fish and sea-food coming out of the clear blue waters of the Mediterranean – we certainly did. He must surely have sat at a seafront table in L'Estaque with a bottle of Rosé as we did here in Cassis.

We came in search of Cézanne and we were richly rewarded on a very full and tiring day that left us immensely satisfied in theming our day around this great painter. I encourage you do the same.

THE STRANGE TALE OF OUR ASCENT OF MT VENTOUX

From early in my life I always had a fascination about the career and death of the British cyclist Tommy Simpson. In my youth I was a keen cyclist but I never cycled competitively. I had one of those 'can you remember where you were when JFK was shot' moments in 1967 when Simpson died that July day during the Tour de France on his ascent of Mt Ventoux. I do remember exactly where I was when Kennedy died, I was in a Fish and Chip shop in Darwen, Lancashire, my home town and clearly remember my parents and everyone around being very shocked. I vividly recall that when Simpson passed away that I was in Blackpool, Lancashire on one of our ubiquitous summer holidays, listening in my earpiece to a cricket commentary on my transistor radio when a newsflash interrupted this very English scene flowing around in my head. I think importantly for me though it was that Simpsons death was the first one in my life that really registered on my consciousness - how could such an athlete just die?

Simpson it is true contributed to his demise due to his response to the extreme pressure to succeed that surrounds the Tour de France and continues to do so to this day. Sadly, it was ever thus, that ways were being found to enhance a rider's performance in the Tour and it was concluded that he also had done so and this had made him go unknowingly beyond the limits of endurance. Due to having been quite debilitating ill in the previous days of the Tour a tragedy was the inevitable consequence. He was, despite joining in with the culture of the times in striving to be better at any cost, a very popular figure and in England he was revered as an athlete which was unusual for the somewhat minority spectator sport of cycling. What I am saying really is that he was not a Soccer playing superstar but through strength of character and that determination to win he had broken through the barrier into much wider popularity. He certainly had with me and I had followed his career avidly and for that reason his death was a massive event in my life. The modern comparison for my son would be the death of Ayrton Senna.

When travelling in Provence I had always looked up at Mt Ventoux, you have to as you cannot miss it, thinking that I must go up there and pay my respects at Simpsons memorial, constructed where he fell, just one kilometre from the summit on the route going up from the village of Malaucène. In 2005 I decided it was high time that I did and so we set out first of all for Malaucène.

We did not go up Ventoux straightaway as there was a morning market on in the town and we spent an hour or so browsing around and as usual we were unable to resist the temptation to buy. After a coffee in the market square we finally set off to start to make our way up Ventoux via the route D974. The road is quite steep even in the early stages leading from Malaucène and you reach a service station looking like an Alps chalet but we passed it by and pressed on towards the summit and our goal for the day. Even early on in our climb up the mountain by car it is clear that to do this on a racing cycle must require a certain almost superhuman strength and without condoning it you can see that many would resort to assistance from whatever source available to try to deal with this immense pressure placed on them by the Tour de France. I cannot comprehend how anyone can attempt this at all but on this day there are a few amateur cyclists, some equipped with oxygen, attempting to emulate their heroes from the Tour. I am not sure how sensible it is to try but try they must.

Our car is new, a Skoda Octavia top of the range diesel model with the larger engine and has never missed a beat in all the time I have owned it as a company car. It has taken us the nearly 1000 miles from the North of England with ease and for the last week we have toured around the area without it offering complaint. The car is in the very best of condition. We round some zig zag bends and bizarrely at a couple of points I have the sensation of going downhill. I have had this feeling occur also in the English Lakes at higher altitude when your car seems to be almost cruising with minimum power being applied. I am sure there must be a scientific explanation of this phenomenon. We carry on uphill quite slowly as I need to concentrate and we hesitantly reach somewhere around 4500 feet in altitude.

It is around this point on the climb and not very far from our objective of Tommy Simpson's memorial that something very strange starts to happen with our vehicle. The car becomes very unresponsive and does not gain any further height with ease, becoming extremely sluggish and you sense that the engine has the signs of overheating and I half expect to see some smoke coming from under the bonnet. This is very much a quite disconcerting sensation, but worse follows in that it now appears to be most of the mechanics of the car that are starting to shut down and not responding to my control. This was quite scary as we were at a high altitude with serious drops going down from the side of the road and I did not feel I was in control of the vehicle even though I was only progressing the car at a very low speed. I decided to ease the car over to the mountain face side of the road and it did so very reluctantly. I was I have to admit shaking and extremely stressed by this as was Niamh.

There was definitely no possibility of me trying to continue up the mountain road as my nerves were completely shot at. It was essential in view of what was going on with the mechanics of the car that we try to get back down the mountain safely. Sadly, I would be thwarted in getting up to Simpsons memorial but discretion is as they say the better part of valour.

I told Niamh to get out of the car while I try to attempt to turn the vehicle around to head back down the mountain road. I have visually checked the engine etc.. and nothing seems on face value to be mechanically amiss with the vehicle. The car really does not want to move but eventually I do manage after about a twenty point turn to safely get it pointing in the opposite direction and Niamh reluctantly gets back in. We start to retrace our steps down Ventoux and come immediately to a sharp turn. I brake and there is absolutely no response from the pedals. Fortunately at this gentler part of the decent we are not going too fast and I negotiate the bend which then straightens out to a long steeper descent. Again I try the brakes and – nothing! I manically pull on the hand brake and point the car to the mountainside and eventually bring it to a stop in a small ditch by the side of the road. Our nerves have been through the wringer and back again.

At this point we both get out and now see our car as a demented enemy no longer the faithful friend that has served us so well thus far. The only plan I can think of is that we bide our time and let the car completely cool down and then hesitantly and conservatively try again. This is what we do and when I am happy that we have left it long enough we get back inside. Heading cautiously down the descent the brakes are not perfect by any means but they seem as if they will get us back to Malaucène if I take considerable care. We slowly but surely do this and it was an incredible relief to get back down and park in the commune, get out and have a double expresso and mop each other's brow. I had been thwarted in my plan for the day but worst of all we had got ourselves into a very serious position on that climb and had felt that it could easily, very easily have ended with a far worse result.

I have no explanation as to what occurred with the car on that mountain road. The altitude and the cars reaction to that height was the only thing that I could put it down to. What made it completely bizarre was that we got back in the car and travelled all the way back to Mazan where we were staying the vehicle drove and responded perfectly as it always had done previously. I couldn't take it to a garage as there was nothing to look at, it was fine. It drove perfectly for the rest of the week and on the long journey back to England.

It was indeed time for a bottle of wine or two. I never got to Tommy Simpson's memorial and reaching it is still on my 'to do list'. I will get there, probably without Niamh, I will pay my respects to my childhood cycling hero but I will do it with great respect for this dangerous mountain and I will do it with care and talk kindly to my car on the way up.

PEOPLE & PLACES – LATER TRIPS TO PROVENCE

Cereste & Mas de la Baou

An area of Provence that is not as fre-quented by tourists as the central part of the Luberon is the area beyond Apt travelling east on the D900 until you arrive at the road to Cereste. For us the selected place to stay here in this village was Mas de la Baou and I genuinely could not have chosen a better spot for a week of rest and relax-ation after a very busy and stressful year back home in England. This large property had once been a collec-tion of old farm buildings of the Provencal Mas type construction and had mainly been in its later years used as accommodation for livestock. It had been pur-chased a few years ago by this lovely couple now in their 60's and they had given these ancient buildings the most amazing transformation. Over a period of only two years this guy somehow did the work all by himself converting this massive house into gites and renovating the larger part as living accommodation for themselves as well as landscaping the large grounds into gardens that were incredibly beautiful. There is a vast intoxicating lavender field that you are able to walk through looking over and taking you right to the village and they had created an organic swimming pool complete with resident frogs. A truly fabulous place.

The other two gites on site were occupied during our stay by two families of Belgium tourists. I don't know about you but I do tend to find the Belgians to be possibly the most non-gregarious people in the world. We did manage to pass the odd 'bonjour' but that was about it as far as stimulating conversation went but in a way entirely due to our need for peace and recovery time this lack of repartee suited us for what was the first week of a long two week trip to the South. One thing that did just rankle with me to a degree was that they took over the B B Q completely for the full week without any consultation. One night I was just heading out to the outdoor kitchen area with my plate of goodies that I had obtained fresh from the market to cook for supper only to find they were just arriving at the kitchen with theirs and had beaten me to it - again. So I gave up after that.

The small village of Cereste has everything you may need for a self-catering stay despite its modest size and it certainly was a lovely short stroll and a fragrant one through the lavender field, Niamh brushing her hand through the flowers as we walked.

You could simply just have remained cossetted on this property all week if you only wanted to enjoy a totally relaxing break.

One day we had a browse around the small market in Cereste village and we noticed the village butcher had some chicken roti starting to cook on the spit and thought that would be just mouth-wateringly perfect for our lunch back in the garden at the mas partnered with a glass of rosé and a view and scent of the lavender fields. Later that morning after our market visit I went to buy said chicken but found that the reaction from all concerned in the tiny shop was all furrowed brows as they stood looking nonplussed at each other until the butcher's wife came over to me shaking her head whilst holding her well-thumbed little black book.

It seemed to me that she was then obviously totting up the orders for chicken that she had in her book and after what seemed to be an eternity frozen in time with me being the object of everybody's fascination - being the Englishman who had the temerity of daring to ask for an unordered chicken - she decided that no, there were none to be spared - I could however have one tomorrow if I wished but only if I put my name down in her little black book. I declined; I could not go in there again.

Fortunately, during our leisurely stroll around the village I had noticed that the local small shop that like all small village shops in France sells everything that a supermarket does also had a small rotisserie out on the front of the shop on a market day. So being satisfied that I had duly embarrassed myself as much as possible anyway that morning I courageously decided I would try again.

Actually as it turned out during my time in this

next shop I really had not peaked as regards embarrassment to myself.

I asked the friendly chap inside the small emporium if it was just possible, perhaps, maybe, please could I have a chicken, please, merci. Well of course I should from my last experience have realised that it is not that simple and he really went for the full deep intake of breath routine and then started pointing out all these other customers in the shop who were in fact roast chicken lovers just like me who were expectantly waiting for these plump succulent beauties to reach peak cooking perfection. These fine loyal and of course local customers of this man, shopping bags at the ready, all looked at me as if I had a sneaky underhand English mission to deprive them of their lunch or had mentioned Waterloo or something equally offensive and low and behold this man also had his little black book and started to have a look at the roll call and so the totting up procedure started all over again. To add to my new found embarrassment he also repeatedly kept going outside with his inventory to look at the chickens and count them, all of which of course ended up with nobody getting served at all in the shop. So inevitably a long queue builds at the till counter with other people wanting to pay for their non-chicken purchases and all fully aware whose fault it was. Anyway he finally and for me very thankfully reaches a decision:

'Oui Monsieur – une poulet pour vous'

Yes, yes there is one for the foreigner but also unfortunately for the non-chicken patrons of his establishment by this time the chickens are at roti cooking perfection and so back outside he goes and starts bringing them in but only one at a time complete with gravy, potatoes etc. Now, you can only begin to imagine how long all this took as French shopkeepers do not just throw your purchase at you and send you on your way. Oh no, they are properly and neatly packed and there was only him in the shop and he was not to be distracted from this process. I was definitely going to be the last to get one so by the time my turn came around other customers had been there for an age keeping up very accusing glances in my direction, which was located somewhere behind a large stand at the back of the store. Time had stood still for me and I would have preferred the ground to have opened up. The very worst of it was that he first served us all with our chickens before attending at all to the non-chicken queue. Washing up liquid has a longer sell by date than his lovingly prepared chicken.

Great chicken lunch though.

This is a really lovely part of Provence and well away from any tourist traps, in fact in the whole time we were in this area of Provence we only saw five other cars with English plates. There was certainly a general lack of visitors, something that was moaned about wherever we went in France.

We went to one of our favourite markets at Forcalquier on Bastille Day and because of that it was doubly busy on the very large sprawling market despite plenty of sore heads from the festivities of the night before. This I can re-emphasise is one of the best markets in Provence if not France.

We as is quite usual had a bit of a run in with a local here as I went to park the car at a spot where we had safely done so on a previous visit and found that the car park area was full but they had conveniently opened more spaces out into a field and so I headed over there. There was a space at the end of a long line of cars and as I shaped to reverse into it Niamh got out checking on the amount of area I had available to get the car into. As I reversed I was sort of aware of something at the side of my car and Niamh started banging furiously on the roof. There was a Citroen at right angles to me going goodness knows where. I ignored him and reversed into the space and he drove off at speed. When I got out Niamh said he had scraped the paintwork of our car and she was right but he clearly was not staying around to discuss it. I can only think he was going to drive around the back of my car having seen another parking space but how and why he felt this was possible was beyond my comprehension. French drivers!

The extensive lavender fields of this beautiful area were at their colourful and fragrant peak and Niamh really loved seeing them at this time of the year and the heady scents are everywhere. With our own lavender field back at the gite you really had the scent of lavender every day and it was astonishingly beautiful and relaxing.

There is just one other incident that is certainly worth recalling from our time in Cereste at Mas de la Baou. When we arrived the owner had warned us to be on the lookout for scorpions – yes really. - and that is definitely not a creature we are used to seeing in England unless it has arrived in a container of bananas. Anyway of course we thought no more about it as it seemed to be a bit unlikely. That was until the very last day of our stay at the mas when as we were just going to bed we saw to our horror that on the wall above the built in cupboards there was indeed the unmistakable shape of a decent sized scorpion. It was clear Niamh was not going to find sleep easy with that creature only a few feet away and if I am honest neither was I. I tried to reach up to it but only succeeded in causing it to fall onto the top of the cupboards and when I got up that high it had disappeared, presumably and I trust back into the stone walls. Again this was a bit disconcerting when you are not absolutely sure where it is now residing. Apparently when our host bought the place as a tumble down ruin it was teeming with scorpions but he said that they were now just down in numbers to the odd one or two that still survive in the incredibly thick walls. I really do hope he finds these stragglers before we make any return visit.

Before we left at the end of the week Monsieur was kind enough to show us around the part of the mas that they had turned into their home. It was incredible, a real feat of love and devotion to have created such a beautiful atmospheric living area from the wreck of a building that they had found on arrival. He showed us the photos taken during the time period of the restoration and I was in awe at their stamina in being able to accomplish this and in so short a time period. The outside wall at one point was built over a huge mound of rock, like a small hill.H explained that this part was the original accommodation for the cows and other livestock and the building was built over this rocky outcrop. This was even he conceded a task too far and he had decided not to try and remove the rock but instead to turn it into a feature of the property and this he had achieved successfully. A truly gorgeous place to live and to stay and we enjoyed our time here immensely.

'CHEESY' BANON
& SURROUNDING
AREAS

Banon on our lunchtime visit had the sound of musicians playing tunes with a leaning to the blues. I could comfortably have stayed in the square in Banon at a table or by the fountain with a carafe of wine and settled there for the afternoon. The thing about musicians in France that you hear playing in the town and village markets is that they are generally really good unlike the ones back home that often simply tend to be a notch up from begging really. Banon has a lovely wine bar – Le Vins au Vert -where they will match wine by the glass to a lovely plate of charcuterie and cheeses etc for a light lunch and I will mention that again - it is a very enjoyable and relaxing way to spend an hour or two..

Banon is a small and unprepossessing village but surprisingly it punches above its weight in being able to provide pleasure for the visitor. It is really a village for locals and although you will certainly find tourists here you will not find that the village is overwhelmed by them, it has retained its character and not turned itself into a place solely to sell overpriced souvenirs. The closest you get to a souvenir here in Banon is probably the goat cheese for which it is justly famous.

I had on one visit headed into Banon to obtain some goat cheese for Niamh to accompany the evening meal. I found a small shop that sells everything but they were particularly proud of the large range of Banon cheese they had on offer. Many of these discs of goat cheese are wrapped in chestnut leaves and look very attractive on the display. Madam was indeed extremely proud of her cheeses and proceeded to lead me through the characteristics of all of those on offer.

I don't actually like Goats cheese – too goaty.

She wasn't to know that and I certainly was not going to tell her so finally the only way out of this was to select a couple and stop her flow of sales patter and prevent any further tastings. She was happy to be of service and impressed that the English wanted to purchase her cheeses and Niamh certainly enjoyed them.

One early morning we headed from Simiane to Banon for the early morning market taking place in the village square. We were so early this day that we nearly got there before the stallholders and these market sellers were still setting up shop. That day we only needed some vegetables for our evening meal back at the gite so we quickly found a local producer with a quality stall and made some small fresh purchases for the meal. The friendly lady brought out a large bag of freshly cut parsley and I instinctively said 'ah merci madam' as she handed them to the local man stood right next to me. Sensing my disappointment (and embarrassment) she offered me some anyway. You have to keep pace on a French market.

The 'Tour de France' was to pass through Banon shortly but you would not have known it, the French are very blasé about their sporting heritage particularly in these rural areas where the locals have more pressing matters such as their next long lunch.

One day after visiting Forcalquier market we were in search of a long lazy lunch as usual and we first of all headed to the small village of Ongles where I knew there was a well recommended restaurant in the village square but it seemed just a bit too busy when we arrived there so we headed on to Banon which was in any case nearer home. At our first choice of Les Voyageurs restaurant in the main square we were pointed without great ceremony to a table on the terrace and waited a reasonable time but the owner had only eyes and conversation for his friends that were holding court around a large table and the two or three young waitresses had very selective attention spans. There was a French couple sat behind us and they got up and left the restaurant without being served and so at the same time we followed them. Don't put up with such service or lack of it – there are so many obliging and caring restaurateurs out there in France.

Lower down the village we had previously walked past the small wine bar, Les Vins Au Vert opposite the tabac and so we decided to check it out because it had seemed to hint that there was food to be had as well. It turned out that we would be very happy that we had made this choice as the service was warm and friendly and prompt and we thoroughly enjoyed a plate of charcuterie, an onion, tomato and courgette tart, three local goats' cheeses and a couscous salad as well as being able to select wine by the glass (one was a fantastic rich Cairanne Red). Coffee was served with cookies from the village patisserie and that rounded off a perfect light lunch.

The wine shop at the back has a superb selection of French wine and we bought a bottle of the Cairanne we had sampled for lunch and also a port-like Banyuls for the winter. The wine display area has the feel of a wine library – very cosy and beautifully laid out. The lovely owners  and staff created a very amiable atmosphere.

While I played the inevitable French game of 'hunt the toilets', Niamh had been stopped by a French motorcycle tourist and she was asked the directions to a village down the valley close to Forcalquier. She explained to the guy straddling his Harley Davidson that her French was not perfect but she then proceeded to give him precise directions in French.

'Mais non, vous parlez francais perfectament'.

I fortunately returned just as he was about to produce a spare helmet and whisk her away.

It had been funny and satisfying on this trip and also on one that we took earlier in the year over to Brittany that we have been mistaken for being French and that really encourages you to keep up with the speaking and continuing to learn the language. It certainly opens a few doors and even if you make a mistake it goes down very well with the locals.

The village of St Saturnin (Tuesday market) has like so many villages and roadsides in this mountainous and slightly remote region a 'Resistants' memorial and the one in this village is particularly well designed and maintained with individual names and places set out on small plaques in the expansive stonework. This one commemorates the particular tragic day of 1st July 1944 when 14 people of the area were killed in and around St Saturin by the German occupiers. You will find these memorials all over this region and if you take a little time to look there are also streets and squares dedicated to these men and women. Some of the memorials are grand as in St Saturin and no doubt funded by public subscription; some will be small and placed by the roadside or a simple individual plaque on a building. On the road to Apt from Banon you will come across these small roadside memorials and it is worth stopping the car and taking the time to reflect on the tragedy surrounding these men and women and realise that this area has a recent dark side also as a counterpoint to its stunning beauty. Yes I accept that you are on holiday and you will not spend your entire time looking for these sites although there is actually a 'route' signed in the area - 'Chemins de la Memoire' - but please take a quiet moment to contemplate when you can.

Cereste, the village that was our home when we stayed for that glorious week was the base of the French poet Rene Char alias Captain Alexander of the resistance and Cereste has a plaque dedication outside his house in the village. Rene Char maintained his cover and survived the war but many of his associates were not as fortunate. The Gestapo based in the hillside village of Viens were particularly active and on a mission to convey a message to Char in Cereste his young colleague Roger Bernard was arrested and subsequently executed. His is a well-remembered and commemorated name in this region. His memorial is located on the Viens road at the Apt/Cereste junction.

If you have interest at all in this dramatic period of French history it is fascinating to try to trace the stories of these local people on the memorials in this region. The stories of these men and women, many very young, have been kept alive since that time and with a little bit of research you will find some remarkable stories behind the names.

As you are travelling these mountain passes and deep woodland roads it is easy to visualize that it is ideal territory to hide and be disruptive to an occupying force but also it is difficult to imagine an area of such beauty being the scene of such terrors.

There is another memorial by a farmhouse track near to our cottage and no doubt is on the site of the death of these men. One can also imagine that patrolling this region for the Germans would have been a frightening prospect as places for ambush are literally everywhere.

This less touristy region is certainly a land of history – fairly ancient as at Simiane la Rotunde and the more recent history in the hills and valleys of this higher part of Provence.

Murs is another small hilltop village and we were not exactly spoilt for choice as regards lunch destinations as Murs has only one restaurant and no shops other than a pottery (forgive me if I missed any) and we decided to eat our lunch at the Hotel Grillon Restaurant. This restaurant was an excellent enforced choice.

Niamh chose the Pork Brochettes accompanied with an oriental sauce and side dishes served on bamboo leaf 'plates' and I had boneless Chicken thighs rolled and flavoured with herbs and Provencal vegetables and boulangere potatoes with layers of squash between the potatoes and once again flavoured with local sun baked herbs.

We both had the sorbet selection to finish the meal and these were so beautifully flavoured and textured and served with liqueur soaked Luberon cherries. A lovely chilled and fruity local rosé went so very well with the meal and we asked for the cork to finish this bottle later after the drive home. Remember the drink drive limit is lower in French than England so if you are having wine with lunch keep it to a small glass or make sure you have a long afternoon siesta before going back on the road.

Service here in this lovely shaded courtyard in

Murs was of the French friendly laid back 'time is not an issue' variety – be warned and get settled.

An unexpected bonus after our lunch was that Niamh was able to pick some ripe figs from trees in a public garden opposite the Mairie and these could become the evening dessert. The lovely views over the surrounding countryside from this high vantage point make Murs well worth a drive up and again you will not be overrun with tourists.

LAVENDER

I will write of the  remarkable expanse of lavender around the Abbey at Senanque just north of Gordes in the chapter 'Our week in Provence' but it is worth briefly pointing out some other areas that should be on your 'must see' list if you are a lover of this beautiful fragrant plant. I appreciate that there are many people for whom a visit to Provence must be made in the lavender season as it is crucial to their experience of the region. My wife Niamh is one of those people.

Our old friend the village of Banon is a good starting point for a lavender tour as around the village are some magnificent lavender fields and a climb to the church at the top of the village will reveal it all in its stupendous glory. If you briefly go out of the village on the D950 in the direction of Forcalquier you can stop and go down one of the minor roads on your left and experience driving as if you are in a lavender field and there are some fantastic photo opportunities.

After that you can then go back through Banon and take the D950 in the opposite direction to Revest du Bion and I am afraid in writing this section on Provence's most famous and beautiful product that it is difficult to stop using all the usual clichés but this route is truly spectacular at this time of year. It is also not a busy route and is usually missed by most of the lavender tourists.

Moving on by the D950 over the plateau to Sault we passed by mile after mile of gorgeous lavender fields. You will find little here in terms of civilization but then you may suddenly come across a roadside stall that begs you to stop. These stalls will be selling honey and specifically lavender honey.

Be warned the produce is not cheap but quality of this standard has to be paid for and it will be a delight to you. This is a spectacular drive via Reveste or you can also experience more of the same sights and smells going around via St Christol and these routes should not be missed. Sault, perhaps the  unofficial lavender capital, is the most incredible destination for views of the lavender fields because you can easily attain the height needed to look down on the patchwork quilt of fields. This road - the D950 and the area to the south east of Banon – however, are I feel probably as good as it gets if you are a lavender junkie.

Most generic tourist guides will generally say to go to Sault if you want to see the lavender and that is certainly true but this lesser known and very quiet route of the D950 is quite incredible.

Field after field of vibrant colours, the air heady with the scent and the expanse of lavender carries on endlessly on the D34 to St Christol and on to Lagarde d'Apt. Quite a quantity in this area also grows wild so your conscience stays clear when you find some lavender to take and dry for home. This route and region are not to be missed and we were there at the  height of the tourist season and we barely neither passed nor saw any other vehicle on the drive around this circuit. Dropping down from this high vantage point (around 3000 feet) to St Saturnin gives you the most stunning panoramas and a deep sense of thanks for being inside your car as you pass the exhausted cyclists breathing in from oxygen cylinders on their way up.

Before leaving the subject of the area around Sault I would also mention that if you have the time or inclination and really it is well worth a special trip at any time there is the most dramatic of gorges on the way back down towards Mazan from Sault. There is no lavender on this route but it will give you an interlude you will never forget. Instead of staying on the

D1 take the D942 towards Monieux and onwards and you will find this lesser known gorge – Gorges de la Nesque. It is barely mentioned in most guide books but I will not attempt superlatives about this gorge but just encourage you to take this route if you have a head for heights and a love of spectacular scenery. Also along the roadside back on the main road from Banon to Sault you have the finest of provencal herbs, drying in the hot sun in the parched ground.

This is the finest 'Thyme in Provence', the most wonderful ingredient to cook with back at your gite or indeed to save for winter cooking. Heady scents they most certainly are.

The area I mentioned south east of Banon going towards Forcalquier has another claim to fame for you lovers of all things fragrant. It is the interesting site that is used by L'Occitane to gather and distil their lavender that they use in the products that grace their outlets around the world. It is very old worldly in appearance, like an old farm in the American plains and not seeming at all to be high tech. If you stumble upon it be sure to get out of your vehicle as you get the most intense concentrated aroma of lavender that you will ever experience. There are as Niamh unfortunately discovered no free samples on offer.

You can find lavender all over Provence but for us this area I have described is the best you will experience and you can for the most part enjoy it in soli-tude. It is worth a special trip in its own right.

DOMAINE DE SAINT-FERRÉOL' AND THE VAR REGION

W e gently made our way up the long driveway to the Domain de Saint-Ferréol and our bed and breakfast accommodation for the next few days. Parking the car alongside a couple of other at the top of the drive I could not readily see the reception area. The front of the Mas has two symmetrical tower like structures with an archway in between leading to a courtyard where in times past you would imagine horses and carts would have brought in the freshly harvested grapes and produce.

As I started to go round the side of this frontage to what appeared to be a much larger part of the Mas I suddenly heard the sound of four substantial paws rushing across the gravel. Suddenly from around the corner came the most enormous Alsatian dog although at first I thought it must be a horse. I like dogs, small and in moderation, in front of this one I stood immobile, transfixed by this ferocious beast as it bore down on me. It was only a couple of yards away from me when it was stopped dead in its tracks as the unseen chain around its neck brought it to a halt. We stared each other down and I was almost thinking that I was ready to taunt it in its failed mission to devour me but I was still too scared and thought better of it.

Madam came round the corner smiling and gave a warm greeting although not as warm as the one her dog wanted to give me and she introduced me formally to my would be assassin. This gigantic beast Hugo would be my constant friend and companion that week, always by my side as I had breakfast in the courtyard and ready to greet me on our return from a day in the Haute Provence. This was a genuine case of 'bark being worse than its bite' and he turned out to be a huge softie and not a killer.

The wine producing Domaine de Saint-Ferréol estate is situated well into the countryside of the Var Department of Provence, between the uplands of the Verdon with its famous gorges and the Sainte Baume and Sainte Victoire mountains. The estate lies on the plain of Pontevès at the foot of the village of that name, with views of the Bessillons mountain peaks. A very pleasant and picturesque location and our room has views up to Ponteves and its medieval castle ruins, which are all beautifully lit up at night giving a spectacular view from our accommodation in the evening.

On the large estate the Jerphanion family grow a mixture of wine grapes and cereal crops. The delicious wines that they produce carry the official designation of origin (AOC) Coteaux Varois de Provence, but also importantly they can make local Pays du Var wines, these offer them more scope to express the terroir of the domain. They are also extremely hospitable to their guests. Monsieur happily explained the way wines were produced on the domain and was very passionate about their quality and heritage. It was most enjoyable to be able to stroll around the large estate and take in the beauty of this area, one that was a new region for us and a contrasting landscape to the Luberon or Vaucluse.

One of the attractions of staying here was that although we were staying as bed and breakfast clients there was a generous separate kitchen area that could be used by the guests. Always one of the most enjoyable features for us when staying and touring in Provence is that you can find a market nearby on nearly every day and you can source produce to prepare in the evening rather than always eating out in a restaurant. It is a real pleasure to be able to find daily such fresh and varied produce and be inspired to create something simple and tasty to be enjoyed on a warm terrace such as the one at this domain.

The second night we were there we had been to the market at Cotignac. This market is not huge but is filled with local produce ranging from fruit and vegetables alongside the very fragrant cured sausages and of course every variety of olive that you can possibly imagine. So we were well stocked and prepared with our tray as we headed downstairs to the kitchen. As I opened the door it was clear from the garlicky aromas coming from inside that someone else had beaten us to it. Standing there were two men who were straight out of Mafia central casting. They looked very surprised to see us - well furtive actually. One thing they most clearly were not - tourists. They had finished cooking so the kitchen was becoming free for us to use but I have to admit I was a little uneasy about cooking while these two characters were eating in the kitchen.

They said they were from Marseille (quelle surprise) and were just here for an overnight stay as they had 'business' in the area. They were extremely amiable but did not ask us anything about who we were or where we were from and I was happy not to enquire as to their profession. As they said, they were on a short stay and once they left the kitchen we did not encounter them again but it was a strange surreal meeting and a tiny glimpse into another different side to the Provence that we come to experience as tourists.

We took the opportunity whilst in the region to drive up to the commune of Moustiers Sainte Marie in the region of the Gorges du Verdon. It is quite a drive to this lofty place and our stay around this area coincided with some of the hottest weather recorded for many years in Provence. This day the thermometer touched 100 degrees (around 40 deg. Celsius). Moustiers is famous for its distinctive pottery and the beauty of its village which is built terrace like against two cliffs. Between the cliffs is suspended a golden star that no one knows the exact origin of but this star seems to date back many hundreds of years and of course has been replaced several times. I wanted a closer look. What a crazy idea, but I decided as Niamh was browsing the shops that I would climb up to get nearer the suspended star, gaining a photo opportunity. I never made it. I got part way and felt that I was in imminent danger of collapse due to the blazing sun and extreme heat. Mad fool. I slowly retraced my steps and staggered around to find Niamh.

We decided it was close enough to lunchtime so we could go and find a restaurant and I could also have some water to cool down. We sat at a terrace table but water was slow to come and I could feel myself getting close to passing out in the heat. We left, found a shop and I slaked my thirst pouring the rest of the contents of the water bottle over my head and revived a little before finding a different restaurant for a light lunch. I learnt a valuable lesson that day and my very next purchase just had to be a more covering sun hat.

The week after we left Provence they had severe wild fires in the area which gives you an idea of how extremely and unusually hot it had been.

I felt physically unable to do a full tour of the Gorges du Verdon but we did a short circuit of the first part and if you are up in the region then you must come and see the remarkable turquoise lakes that dot the area throughout the gorges. A breath-taking scene is before you and if you have a head for heights and dangerous high roads then you will be greatly rewarded by taking the full route. We however headed back to the Domain and I was a little wiser than when I had set out to explore this extraordinary hill country. And yes, we did buy some pottery and we still have it on display today. Tourists!

A slightly easier although still quite hilly drive is up to the commune of Tourtour, one of the 'Plus Beaux Villages de France'. Tourtour is very beautiful, not just the village but the stupendous views all around you that stretch to the Mediterranean sea and to Montagne Saint Victoire, Cézanne's favourite subject. We had a light lunch on the route that leads from the village up to the old Romanesque St Denis church that dominates and keeps a watchful eye straight down into the village. This road has some fine sturdy old plane trees and many tempting places to sit under a parasol and enjoy the shade with a cold drink.

I used 'les toilettes' in the lunchtime restaurant before we left. Many years ago Michael Palin made his first tourist film for the BBC and in it he concluded his train journey up in the west coast of Scotland and was filmed sitting at a window table in his hotel having breakfast. He commented that if he was to make a series of 'Greatest Breakfast Table Views of the World' then this was surely one of them. My view from the open window of the loo was undoubtedly one of the 'Greatest views from a toilet in the world'. Never forgot it.

As we strolled up to the church its heavy wooden doors suddenly creaked open and we were swiftly engulfed by a crowd of excited children and their parents. This colourful noisy scene was the end of a mass confirmation ceremony and we were placed in the middle of it all. We made our way through the throngs of people and sat at the side of the church for a while. The views were incredible and as the hum died away and as they all made their way into the village the priest closed the ancient wooden doors, walked into the village for his lunch and we sat and enjoyed the peace and the panorama of the region spread out before us. Later on reflecting the tourists that we were we bought a ubiquitous yellow and blue/green olive pattern Provencal table cloth – it is still in use.

Madam made one specific recommendation for a location for us to pay a visit to and that was to go to the nearby village of Sillans la Cascade. It was not to see the village, pretty as it may be but for the other dominant feature and the clue is in the name. The waterfall you will find is along a shady woodland path of about just over half a mile that gives no hint of what is to come at the end of the stroll. You become aware of the gentle splash of water that gets louder as you walk towards it and a slight humid haze in the air. The sight that greets you is a truly stunning waterfall that cascades into a turquoise lake below. The waters are very cold and clear and some do swim but the access to the water is a little difficult and not recommended. The sight and sensory experience of being in this beautiful cool amphitheatre is surely reward enough. You will find it generally peaceful here as it is one more of Provence's lesser known sights but one that demands a visit if you are in this Var region of Provence.

We headed back to the Luberon after our stay at the Domain, our car well stocked with the wines of Saint Ferréol, with lovely memories of a different area of Provence and our lovely hospitable hosts - and Hugo the dog.

RESTAURANTS

This section on one of my favourite topics is intended to give to you just a small flavour of what we have experienced over the years in this beautiful and plentiful region of France. I have also mentioned other restaurants and cafes in different sections of the book. It is not intended to be a guidebook but I hope all our experiences enable you to make some informed choices of your own. That is the best way to experience Provence – find restaurants for yourselves. Yes of course there is Trip Advisor to fall back on these days and I have to say I use it myself but the best finds will always be the ones that you choose and particularly if you try to observe where the locals are eating. If a restaurant is empty and does not fill up then there is probably a reason for that and the locals know it. Avoid like the plague the charming waiter with a menu that has photos for the English speaker and be open minded – if it looks, smells and feels right then it probably is. Enjoy your lunch.

LA FOURCHETTE RUE RACINE AVIGNON

L a Fourchette is our restaurant of choice for lunch when in Avignon and for the very good reason that the food is sublime and the service and ambiance just perfect. We were strolling around one early morning on our very first visit to Avignon and stumbled upon it situated just off the Place de l'Horloge. The outside of La Fourchette belies the lovely interior and that end of the street is narrow and unexciting but do go in, it is well worth it to enjoy one of the best dining experience we have had in Provence.

On that first visit it was the menu 'prix fixe' designed for lunch that caught our eye with the promise of fresh fish and some lovely desserts. It was only around ten thirty in the morning and the door was open so I decided to reserve a table for lunch. The young man was very welcoming but had difficulty understanding my name but for that I totally understand as I have to repeat it constantly in England to be understood. I could not really say as I am always inclined to do – 'as in the cricketer' here in Southern France (if not English then please Google). An imposing lady who appeared to be the owner, very expensively dressed, embellished and coiffured, came over to reception and at that point I took his pen and reservation book from him and wrote the booking in it myself for a 1 o'clock table for lunch. She smiled and said she would look forward to seeing us later. La Fourchette is owned and run by the Hiely family who have other interests in restaurants in Avignon and have been serving the people and visitors of Avignon for generations. Their signature restaurant Hiely Lucullus is not far from here and is a fine dining destination in Avignon.

Walking into to the restaurant reception at the arranged time we were given a warm welcome and shown to our table which was a good one near the windows that open up wide in the hot July heat. If you were unsure of the name of the restaurant then you are left in no doubt by the quantity of forks of many varieties that adorned the walls. The décor is just right for a restaurant of this type and just like the service is unfussy but professional and warm.

Placed on the table was a chilled carafe of white wine from just north of Chateauneuf de Pape and we ordered our mains. These were superb, dourade served with a warm tomato and herb sauce and scallops seared to perfection with a Provençale salad. The desserts were artistic perfection on a plate and of course made use of the fresh fruits of the region.

At the start of our meal as we were enjoying our wine and waiting for our main courses to be prepared two elegant and immaculately dressed ladies arrived, looking every inch as if they had just been beamed in from Paris. The restaurant was reasonably full but there appeared to be a couple of tables still unused. From the outset these two ladies came across in demeanour as being quite haughty and behaved almost of if they should have been recognised as being 'somebody'. Our owner lady is a woman who is confidently and proudly in charge, a woman that knows the family product on offer is superb and she is proud of it and certainly not fazed by any 'attitude'.

You want a table, then please ask nicely as it is a pleasure to eat here and they would like you to treat them with the respect you would give if you are entering their home and there is nothing wrong with that.

She asks 'Madam, have you made a reservation?'

'Non' is the curt reply

'Then I have not got a table available' she smiled. And yes she really did smile.

'Good for you', I thought and was glad that I had taken the time and had the courtesy to reserve a table. Yes, you may say that we are the customer and they are providing the service so should be glad just to take the money and serve such people. It doesn't really work like that in France. In a good French restaurant you should feel that you are a guest rather than a customer and the proprietors do expect you to behave as if that is the case. If you do then you not only have a great dining experience but you leave as friends. That's how it works and long may it be that way. It is not that they are being snooty as is so often the complaint rather it is in the main that they are not treated with respect as potential friends that will be glad to serve you perfectly well for many years if you reciprocate correctly to them. This is such a restaurant.

We have been back to La Fourchette every time we have come to Avignon and have taken friends there also. It is one of the best in my opinion and a restaurant that I can and will wholeheartedly recommend to you.

LA FIACRE

O ne day out
on our meandering travels
and more than ready for a
lunch away from the hot
Provencal sun we decided

on the restaurant of Le Fiacre just outside the village
of Goult on the N100 heading to Apt.

To the rear of the restaurant they have a tree
shaded terrace outside a large Provencal Mas, a setting
that is a very attractive place to dine despite the Mistral wind whipping up a fair amount of dust from time
to time.

The meal and setting were exactly what we had
travelled so far to find and sustain us through the
coming English winter.

From the outset you knew it was going to be good
when you are immediately given olives and other nibbles and served with drinks and a pre-starter course
to settle you into what is sure to be a long leisurely

lunch.

The meal and experience just got better when we were served with incredibly fresh starters of tomatoes with smoked salmon dressed in a citrus olive oil dressing and goats cheese soufflé with grilled aubergines, courgettes etc..

Mains were a perfectly roasted duck breast accompanied with polenta and Provencal vegetables and a dish of baked flakingly fresh cod with aioli.

Refreshing deserts of Ice cream, tuilles and melon with cherry sorbet all soaked in Beames de Venice sweet wine finished it off. Perfection.

It reminded us of the episode of the US sitcom Frasier where Niles and Frasier are ecstatic that they managed to pick a tiny flaw in their 'perfect' evening dining experience – that they said was the best bit for them.

We tried to find a flaw but failed – it really had to be a perfect ten. Having said that I thought they were going to blow all the good work at the end of the meal as the coffees had nothing to accompany them – but no, some excellent tuilles and meringues appeared as if by magic and all was well. Lovely service as well with everything done with a smile.

We repeated the experience about two years later

and I will tell of that in the final chapter of this book.

We had thought for a while about coming here again as the last time was so perfect and to have been disappointed perhaps by a new chef or new owners or just a drop in standards would have spoilt any previous memory of the restaurant. If anything it was even better this time around and you could see that hard work had gone into trying to make the dishes even more attractive and flavoursome.

It seems though that the chef proprietor and his charming wife have recently moved on. So if anyone knows where they are recreating the joys of La Fiacre please let me know.

LE FOURNIL
BONNIEUX

L e Fournil is  one of our very favourite restaurants and we have been coming here for many years. It is to be found in Place Carnot, a very small square in Bonnieux blessed with an outside terrace set around a fountain. As Jane Austen would have said of the restaurant - 'it is happily situated'. The interior of the restaurant is actually cut into the rock face on which the higher part of town and the church at the top of the hill are located.

This is always a busy restaurant because of its location and the simple fact that the food and service are extremely fine. The basis of the cooking and menu here is French classical food of the south done simply and using the freshest of local ingredients. My type of place.

For me I would always reserve a table on the terrace rather than inside when dining in fine weather. There is nothing that contributes to a feeling of well-being than a long French lunch on the terrace accompanied by a chilled local wine. This is a restaurant and location that provides that feeling as good as anywhere you may find in France. There is such a lovely contented hum about the place on a warm summer day with the happy diners being served effortlessly by the easy going waiters and owners.

On the Autumn day of writing this the lunch menu is :

Roast quail, port jus, celeriac and sweet onions

Fish of the day

Ox cheeks braised in red wine, slow roast autumn vegetables

This gives you a flavour of how the local produce is used as per the season and the simplicity of the cooking, nothing fancy ensuring that your plate is not presented as confused by the chef being too clever with too many extra ingredients.

On our last visit Niamh had a beautiful piece of

cod roasted to perfection with leeks and very smooth buttery cheesy mash potatoes. I had the very tenderest and flavoursome cut of pork tenderloin with sage sauce and petit pois. The deserts were chocolate and raspberry with local ice cream. A sublime lunch.

We had a bottle of rosé wine from a winery called Chateau La Canorgue, a maker that the label on the bottle indicated was a local domain. The waiter explained that it was just off the Route Pont Julian going back down the hill towards the old Roman bridge.

Being in a lovely chilled world of my own coming to the end of the long relaxing lunch I had not picked up on something that in retrospect was actually quite obvious.

The charming attentive waiter was giving far more attention to me than to Niamh.

She finally pointed it out to me and I just laughed it off saying that I was not THAT attractive. We ordered coffee and he brought Niamh's and set it down without fuss but serving mine he just slightly spilled some coffee into the saucer. His apologies are just a little too profuse than necessary but I said it was:

'OK, pas un problème monsieur'.

No, he absolutely insisted that the cup must be

changed and he was all over me like a rash. He went off to the bar to bring a fresh cup and Niamh just laughed. My eyes had been opened and I just hoped he would not slip me a note with his number on it on returning as I really wanted to spend the rest of the day with Niamh and not have to let him down gently.

Mmm, that was a French lunch.

Anyway, flattered as I was, Niamh and I left together after gushing farewells and headed off down the hill to find Chateau La Conorgue. This turned out to be the chateau where 'A Good Year' starring Russell  Crowe was filmed and we had an excellent visit to round off another memorable lunch at Le Fournil, a location that also appears in that movie.

AUBERGE DE
LA LOUBE

S adly, at the time of writing I believe this unique restaurant at Buoux has just closed its doors but I have to include it here just to give you the experience of what this extraordinary man Maurice achieved here in this tiny village. I had heard of this place via my usual research but it was our painter friend Francoise in Rousillon that told us we had to eat here as Maurice was a friend of hers and we would not regret it as it was a little bit different and a special place. She also said that Maurice was retiring and this was his last year so we should go and experience this restaurant while we could. She was not wrong with that advice although in the event Maurice ran the restaurant for another 10 years or so.

One of few buildings in the tiny village of Buoux this restaurant has an initial appearance of perhaps being stables and he indeed has a large collection of carriages and equine related items. The dining area is very casual and almost appears as if you are just in someone's rural house and terrace.

We were greeted warmly although little English is spoken, well none actually. The uniqueness of this restaurant is that it has a speciality dish, or rather dishes plural that I have never seen done elsewhere. You are served a selection of 16 small dishes, a little like tapas but smaller and placed on a large tray. Niamh decided to have this feast and I conservatively ordered a succulent slow cooked lamb dish and ate that as I watched her trying to get through this incredible selection of small dishes. Some were savoury, some vegetable, olives, tapenade, marinated cheeses and served with homemade crusty bread. It was quite a sight to behold. Niamh really enjoyed most of the plates and some not quite as much and I tried a few of them myself to help out in trying to clean the plates and not offend Monsieur.

It has to be said that this was not French gastronomy at its absolute pinnacle but it was a wonderful take on producing French Tapas and giving you time to enjoy a long leisurely and varied lunch experience. One did have to wonder just how he managed to do this every day as there appeared to be very few if any more cooks in the restaurant and how he managed to get such a variety of produce up to this remote place high up in the Luberon. It was one lunch we will remember for a very long time so thank you Francoise.

We sat for a while on the edge of the village taking in the extensive rolling views and dozing a little to let the wine weave its magic and were well satisfied. Buoux is a very small place but the drive up is well worth it and you can come or go via Saignon or Bonnieux to enjoy this remote high plateau and look down over the Luberon valley.

LE PISTOU - CHATEAUNEUF DU PAPE

T his restaurant I can honestly say was in fact a Trip Advisor inspired choice on the street leading up to the old Chateau as in Chateauneuf du Pape. I know you are going to say that it does not look high class or fancy and in-

deed it is not and does not pretend to be. What it is though is a friendly honest bistro type restaurant that serves quality cooking with local ingredients at a very fair price. This is a gem of a find in an expensive wine village. It just has the air of a place that knows what it is and knows how to accomplish what it sets out to achieve for its customers very well indeed. A confident and friendly place.

If you can get a table on the small terrace you will have the added bonus of people watching as wine lovers stagger up the hill to pay their respects to the symbol of great French red wine at the top of the village. Funnily enough I always assumed that the Chateau was still occupied and you would have to pay to have a visit to look around it and its contents. That is not that case as most of you probably know. It is in fact more of a well preserved ruin behind that famous façade. It is though worth making that trip to the top as the chateau is interesting and the views especially back down the Rhone River towards Avignon are splendid. There are more restaurants also for you to peruse.

Le Pistou serves a generous and well executed prix fixe lunch and with a bottle or carafe of wine will not disturb your wallet too much.

As I said we really decided on Le Pistou because of the reviews and I can reiterate that this is worth a detour for lunch. The fixed price menu on offer on this day was superb, very fresh local ingredients that were cooked skilfully and at a price that truly makes you wonder how they do it. We had all three courses from the fixed price menu with both of us choosing the chicken fricassee for the main course which was outstanding - packed with Provencal flavours and very falling apart tender. There is a good range of excellent local wines at an affordable price to complement your meal. The overall service was charming and they cheerfully accommodated whoever called from young families, older couples or cyclists. They were especially accommodating to the children in a couple of the parties and made them very welcome. Overall just to reiterate, Le Pistou is situated on a quiet street leading up to the ruined château, the terrace is a very pleasant place to have lunch. From me it comes highly recommended.

Chateauneuf and the countryside around it is a place that the Popes recognized as being the crème de la crème as regards wine production in this region. It is still the same today and is not the place for a bargain if you want the real deal as it were of this premium French wine. It is clearly a place where 'money' congregates but there are other local wines on offer at excellent quality and good value in some of the many cellars that are open to visitors.

At the high end hotel in the centre of the village I came across a famous French soccer player, now a team manager, as he came out of the hotel with a glamorous lady on his arm, presumably his wife, although he is French. It is not really the done thing to whip my camera out and take a photo in his face but they strolled a little and then sat in the pleasant square chatting for a while so I took a photo from a distance. I zoomed in on the photo when I was back home to show my son who agreed that it was indeed the man himself but seemed unimpressed that I appeared to have been stalking him. No more celebrity chasing for me then.

CAFÉ DU SPORTS
SABLET

I n most villages in
France you will find a bar
or café that is the beating
heart of that village, the
place where the locals gravitate towards day and
night. Maybe they go just for a beer and to watch the
racing or soccer on the TV or to have a coffee with
a friend or a bite to eat at lunchtime. A friendly place
where a local resident will stop and chat to a friend
who is eating or drinking on the terrace. A place that
is fun and lively and the language spoken will most
certainly be French. A place where the menu is simple, there are always French fries to be had and often
as here in Sablet there is a Pizza oven. A place where
the welcome is warm and friendly for tourists and locals alike. It will not be a restaurant for fine dining
where you must be overdressed for the occasion. It

will not hurt your wallet unduly but the meal will be tasty and generous and leave you satisfied and happy. You will feel much better for the visit. Café du Sports in Sablet is such a place and these café/bar/restaurants are well worth seeking out.

This restaurant is a venue where there is a genuine air of conviviality which seems to infect everyone in the bar or on the terrace. You will for a certainty be talking to the people at the table next to you within a short period of time after sitting down and I guarantee you will be smiling or laughing with them even though you may not have understood a word any one of you has said.

The terrace offers people watching in the sense that you will see how the villagers in a small place such as Sablet interact, what makes a community like this tick and thrive. You will see the older people from the retirement village come to sit out in the square and old friends go to talk to them. The owner of the Café Bar will be working the tables and shaking hands and chatting to old friends and new customers alike. The bar will be busy but sat out on the terrace it is just a happy muffled sound in the background.

The meal will be simple, a chicken dish, a salad, an entrecote steak and always a side of French fries.

The dessert will be a simple French classic, perhaps an apple tart or floating islands. Always there will be a reasonably priced carafe of the local house wine. A coffee to finish. All exceptional value.

These places are everywhere and OK I accept that you will not drive miles out of your way to go to one but if you are in the area then they are a vital part of your French experience. Give them a try and if you are near Sablet head for the centre of the village and Café du Sports.

This is just a small flavour of the variety of restaurants and cafes that you can find out there if you take your time and seek them out. Some restaurants close down and others can gain new owners or chefs or the chef loses heart and turns it into a burger joint. So don't be too disappointed if you discover that your favourite restaurant is not the same on your next visit, just look again and you will find another great lunch spot in Provence. One feature of Provence that will never change and always repay you amazingly is the markets that you will find in every village and town. You don't need to eat out in Provence every day so make sure of a great meal by going to the market and prepare it yourself just like a local. With a bottle of chilled rosé wine that is perfection in the sun.

A WEEK (OR SO)
IN PROVENCE

F or us one out-standingly memorable visit to Provence was to an old farmhouse near St Simeon La Rotunde stay-ing at a most lovely welcoming gite called La Buisson-ade run by a young couple - Veronique and Enverico. We had stayed here two years previously but on this second trip we really got the very best out of this quiet region of Provence and it was made extra special as we were returning as friends. This trip is from the summer of 2011 and as I will recount the week in some detail in more of a blog style it will be a long chapter so as to take our story day by day. I think this will give you a full flavour of how to enjoy a trip to this beautiful region and round out the whole experience of making the long journey. I do hope you enjoy reading of our experiences and that it will inspire you to travel to this special region of France.

This is our Week in Provence.

Thursday 14th July

Setting off in the early evening from our home in Lancashire to make an overnight stop in a Travelodge Hotel near to Stevenage in Kent to shorten the early morning journey we would need to make to enable us to catch the ferry over to France we easily found the small village in which the hotel was allegedly located. We drove around the small village at least three times without any sign of it other than Niamh continually reminding me that she had pointed out on first entering the village that it was - 'down there'. It was of course, but at least we explored all the possibilities. Not happy!

We went to bed very tired but on turning out the lights I found that there was located above my head green and red flashing lights – a smoke detector. I of course assumed it must be needing new batteries and not wanting to disturb the reception I simply disconnected it and started off to sleep again only for a loud knock coming to our door about five minutes later.

The lady on reception had been disturbed by her fire alarm panel sounding off as I had apparently taken out of action the entire hotel fire alarm system. The lights were 'a feature' and all the hotel smoke alarms were like that so 'would I please not disconnect them'? Not happy!

I was at a loss as to why anyone would design a fire alarm with flashing lights as being suitable for a hotel bedroom – it is beyond me but it had to go back in situ and merrily flashed away in multi-coloured splendour. We slept well anyway.

Friday 15th July

We awoke early at around 5 am and got back into the car to begin the journey to the ferry at Dover which was about an hour and a half distance away. The reason we needed to make this early start was because of the British Open Golf tournament being held at the Royal St Georges course at Sandwich near to Dover and consequently we expected some traffic delays. Thankfully we only had just a fairly brief hold up with the additional golf traffic near to Folkestone and soon we were loaded on to the Calais Ferry. It turned out to be an easy calm crossing but also a noisy one in the company of a large school party who were well behaved but excited – like us.

Our stopover hotel I had chosen on travelling to the South was the Ibis Hotel at Nuits St Georges in the Cote d'Or region of Burgundy. This is very much the centre of French wine country and it was a fairly long drive from Calais making us pretty tired when we arrived thankfully without having any incident or delay on the AutoRoute.

On checking in at the hotel and being English we are always amazed at what you find for your money at these places. We were allocated a spotless well equipped room with an excellent bathroom and we were greeted with the most charming efficiency by the young lady on reception and she easily persuaded us to book a table in the restaurant that evening. Why is it that in France at the hotel check-in desk you feel you are entering into a deep and meaningful relationship that then sadly comes to a sudden end when she hands you the key?

These type of hotels we know from past experience are always good and this one in Nuits St Georges would not be a disappointment.

The important necessity for us first of all though is a shower and siesta and we followed this with a pleasant stroll around this famous old Burgundian wine village. Nuits St Georges was bustling, streets thronged with people, with most of the restaurants open and busy, their tables spilling out onto the street and a colourful musical event taking place in the town square.

The many wine shops and producer domain outlets competed for trade and it made you wish that you could stay longer in such a friendly and cultured place but exploring Burgundy would have to wait for another trip. Despite all the tempting wines on offer actually buying  any would have to wait until we got to Provence, the wines from that Southern region were our priority for purchasing on this trip.

As we expected our dinner that evening back at the hotel was excellent – Jambon Persillé, that speciality ham terrine of the Bourgogne region, was my choice to start the meal and for Niamh it was a cheese and tomato salad. She was then served a splendid pan fried Pave de Saumon in a Beurre Blanc sauce and I decided as I often do in these places to order a Steak frites. As is usual in France my steak was served as just the right side of dead – just.We were far too tired, in fact exhausted, to stay at the table for a dessert, we just managed an expresso coffee and then off to bed and we slept well, very well.

Saturday 16th July

I had decided to set off even earlier than we usually do because I had come up with a cunning early start plan to beat the French to the sun.

Apparently the French motorists had been tipped off about me and already knew I had this plan and the French cars were already on the AutoRoute despite it being still very dark and the time only 4.45am. Thankfully for us the traffic did eventually thin out and we were able to race through the heart of Lyon (must stay here sometime) and finally got into Provence at around 9am. In the end the early start strategy had worked well.

We had one amusing incident on the way down the AutoRoute when we arrived at the Lyon toll booths where Niamh handed the exact toll money over and the attendant said:

'C'est un dix franc' handing straight back to her a Euro like coin.

The offending coin was indeed 10 old francs and we apologized profusely and quickly handed over a proper euro coin naturally assuming that he would realise we had been swindled by a French trader who had slipped it to us somewhere en-route.

But not a bit of it.

As we looked up to him at the toll booth window we got the full disdainful 'Frenchman on the Battlements' scene from Monty Python treatment, we were to him clearly guilty as charged and obviously trying to deceive an official of the French republic – no cheery au revoir here – we were to him most certainly deceitful Anglais.

This turned out to be not our only embarrassing encounter with the French Toll Booth system on this journey to the south. When we came to the exit toll booth at Orange Niamh wound the window down but there was not an attendant to be seen – exit from the AutoRoute turned out to be by carte de credit only, no cash and no assistance.

With other cars coming up to us from behind and there only being this one exit toll booth it meant that

I had to hastily get out of the car and run around the front to the passenger side, quickly get my bearings with this complex machine and fire in the toll ticket and my credit card, hopefully in the correct slots – the barrier then opens instantaneously – I have to then run back around the front of the car and try to drive through the raised barrier before it decides to come down again, and also multi task in trying at the same time to shut the driver's door. I am left in no doubt that we must be a great source of amusement to the French waiting behind us but I decide not to bother looking in my rear view mirror and simply speed embarrassingly away.

We decided that from Orange we will make our way across country taking us down as far as Apt because we were staying quite nearby and the town has a large Saturday market for us to visit. What a market it is. We could not park the car anywhere as the town was absolutely packed with shoppers and we got to the point of being on the verge of giving up trying and driving away from Apt when we turned a corner on the edge of the market at the same time as someone was reversing their vehicle out of a space – great timing.

The scale of Apt market was overwhelming, it is

one of the largest and best in Provence, especially as we were tired from our early start and the journey south but you knew as you looked and walked around that you had definitely arrived and you were truly immersed in the sights, sounds and smells of Provence.

It is a life enhancing feeling to experience - you know in that moment that it has been worth making the effort of driving that long distance from the North of England. It felt  especially so when after browsing on the market for some time we drove along the winding road up the steep hillside from Apt to reach the small village of Saignon for our lunch.

Since our previous visit to Saignon there now appears to be a couple of new restaurants but both of these were closed this Saturday lunchtime. Auberge de Presbytere is open and was the restaurant that we had dined at on the lovely shaded terrace around the fountain during our last visit and this Auberge is excellent but a little expensive for a tired traveller that is really just looking for sustenance - a fuel stop. Across the way, we saw that the Maison de Solveig had a lovely shaded terrace and was already starting to fill up with lunchtime diners so we made that the location for our meal. All the diners seated on the terrace were French – always a good sign and the meal was indeed lovely. Niamh had a 'Saignon' salad and I had some marinated Chicken brochettes with rice with a Pannacotta and a Chocolate dessert to follow.

The meal was certainly very good value and well presented on the plate and we had good service from our friendly young waitress with the 'smiling sheep's head with flower in mouth tattoo' on her ankle. I could I suppose have asked her the significance of that quirky de-sign but thought the better of it. The young lady was kind enough to ask if we were French or English so she must have been of the opinion that our efforts at the French language were more than acceptable.

There was seated opposite our table on the terrace an elderly lady in a large Parisian party and she chose the same chocolate dessert that I had ordered.

Like mine this has been presented to her with a small pot of marmalade to compliment the chocolate and cream and I found that this combination worked very acceptably together. Clearly though this assembly of ingredients was not something she had ever seen in Paris and she held the small pot of marmalade up and asked round the table as to why it was there. With nobody in her party any the wiser she just decided to spoon it down in one on its own and seemed quite content with the resulting taste sensation.

As we made our way back through the pretty village of Saignon to our car we were feeling very satisfied in the warmth of the summer sun and headed back down the winding road into the valley at Apt and onwards into the hills on the other side towards the small village of Simiane le Rotunde to our holiday cottage to reunite with Veronique, Enverico and Tyson the Rottweiler.

In fact, we were still a little early despite the distance we had travelled and having also taking time to fit in a long French lunch so we passed the farmhouse gite by and drove on to the village of Banon to pick up a few provisions for the evening.

This time I would try not to be persuaded, as had happened to me on a previous visit, to buy more

Banon Goat cheese than we could possibly use. Sure enough the sales pitch in the same little grocery store was in full charming flow but this time I maintained my cheesy discipline and bought only the items on my list of essentials and that is of course mainly wine. There are  some things that appear to have changed since our previous visit to this little village, the wine shop has gone and a new restaurant has opened next to the wine bar. I was pleased that there was still the same friendly contented hum about the place as the afternoon headed towards siesta time. I left the village before I fell asleep myself.

We turned into the drive of La Buissonade and parked the car only to see three people emerging from OUR cottage. Please no, surely we weren't double booked, simply your worst nightmare after travelling so far and being so very tired. Fortunately not, my mental crisis instantly over, Veronique had changed her hair colour and looked very different on first appearance from remembering her from our last visit and she just had a friend with her who was helping her to clean the cottage, Veronique having been late back from delivering a consignment of finished goods from their food business over to a client some distance away in the Luberon.

She warmly greeted us and gave us a very welcome cool drink as we waited at the garden table for her to finish the final touches to our gite and then we quickly and thankfully settled in to our Provencal home for the next week.

Since our last stay the family have gained a new Rottweiler puppy called Ganache and she quickly decided that she wanted to wrap her teeth around my leg or arm, in a playful way of course (I think), and fortunately Enverico soon restored some doggy discipline. I can see we, well especially me, will not have seen the last of Ganache this coming week.

Veronique says it will rain tomorrow; it says so on her computer – surely not.

We have a small meal of produce we purchased in Banon of melon, ham and tomatoes with local rosé wine before a good long restorative sleep.

Well, that's what we thought.

Just after midnight at around 12.30 we heard

the sounds of an approaching squadron of helicopters coming down the valley plain. The cacophony of sound was very much like the assault on your senses in one of those films where the Americans marines storm in and carry out a daring rescue missio. Bravely looking out into the darkness it turned out that it was only the neighbouring farmer and his squadron of friends working in the fields with a battery of combine harvesters.

He had decided no doubt because of Veroniques' dismal weather forecast, that it was imperative that he harvested the wheat in the surrounding fields right now. We eventually had to be thankful that he and his workforce fortunately only carried on with his mission until 3am! Rural France is so peaceful.

Sunday 17th July

It is raining. This actually is the very first time on all of our trips to Provence that we have experienced rain. The downpour did not last for very long on that first morning but the day did stay fairly dull but also extremely warm. We had only one priority today, with our not being quite as restored in energy as we would have liked - to have a good long lunch. First of all we headed back down the valley to Apt and then over to the village of Menerbes and visually checked out two restaurants. One of these particularly has had good recommendations, La Veranda, but somehow seeing the restaurant it did not inspire with a fairly pricy menu just for Sunday lunch and the waiting staff resplendent in tee shirt uniform didn't on this occasion give off a welcoming or inspiring ambiance. The restaurant was also not overly busy either despite there being very little competition in the village. This was a time when your mood and instinct says leave it and move on. (We actually had lunch here a few years later and it was superb) The next door restaurant to La Veranda was full apart from a single table near to the draughty front door and this one seemed more like the type of place we were looking for. If they had had another better positioned table available then we would have stayed in the village and eaten there. We took the car across the side of the valley gaining height up to the hillside village of Bonnieux and we walked around for a while checking the various menus before arriving at Le Fournil restaurant. The fine terrace around the fountain in the village square looked sad with its upturned tables placed so because of the wet weather and it was difficult to see if the restaurant was even open despite a menu being chalked on the board. We have been turned away from Le Fournil before having arrived without a reservation but thought we would ask at reception anyway and try our luck. 'Bien sur' said the patron and led us upstairs to the last table in the 'cave' part of the building.

This restaurant is built right up against the rock face in the lower part of the village and the interior is excavated right into the side of the hill. The upstairs seating area does feel a little claustrophobic but is slightly brightened by the windows looking down onto the square. Le Fournil has a lovely ambiance to it with attentive and friendly waiters who do like to please with their well-rehearsed but effortless service.

Niamh had the fish plat du jour of Merlu and I decided on the lamb cooked 'a point'. Both dishes were superb. I followed the lamb with an exquisite chocolate cake with red fruits and berry sauce and Niamh had the soft cheese Fromage Blanc she so loves to have as a simple dessert in France. It was dull and cloudy outside and we lingered at the table and finished our local bottle of rosé wine and then ordered coffees and we felt very satisfied that we were properly 'in France'.

We were the last diners out of the restaurant and after we had settled the bill Monsieur locked the door behind us and we headed for a stroll up to the old church high above the restaurant. There are spectacular views all around you from this high vantage point and at that perched situation on the hillside you can see the whole Luberon plain stretched out before you. Bonnieux is indeed a special village and we love it for unlike some other villages in the Luberon it is relatively not as commercialised and can be much less crowded with tourists- it has space to move and breathe in its narrow streets and high places.

On the way back home we headed out of the village down the long road back into the Luberon plain to pay a visit to the Cave de Bonnieux local wine cooperative and we were as is usual here treated to the requisite wine tasting before buying a few varied bottles of wine to enjoy during the week. Perhaps we will come back later to get some more for home - of course we will. They also sell wine from the pump here as well as bottled– these from the pump are at amazing prices of around 1.70 Euros a litre. The quality even with these volume wines is excellent here so you really can't go wrong and you certainly feel you have got great quality wine at a very fair price.

Doubling back on the road heading towards Bonnieux we turned left towards Pont Julien, the ancient limestone Roman Bridge that is still standing firm and usable even today after all these centuries. This bridge is much smaller, well very much smaller, than the world 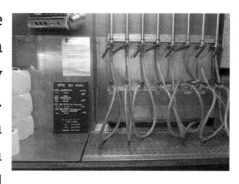 famous Roman Pont du Gard, although you still have before you a remarkable feat of ancient architecture and with the River Calavon that it spans now running at just a tiny trickle it does seems a bit of over-kill for the effort that must have been involved over two thousand years ago. It was still used until fairly recently for car traffic which is remarkable but now you and your car pass close by on a new bridge. The ancient bridge is well worth a detour and a chance to lose yourself in your imagination of a distant past when the Romans poured in to occupy and develop the area on the Via Domitia.

So now back to home for a siesta and a quiet light supper.

Monday 18th July

We awake and throw open the curtains on a truly glorious day although perhaps a touch cooler than we would normally have expected for July in Provence. I am not complaining however as the temperature is better suited to our English constitutions.

After a drive through beautiful lavender filled countryside from Banon we arrived early at Forcalquier market, this surely one of the very best markets in Provence if not in all of France. Parking your car here can be a nightmare but the early start we had wisely made had paid off and we parked our vehicle quickly and easily. It was lovely and cool on the streets and many traders were still setting up their stalls in this ancient and slightly faded provincial town. It is a French town of course but Forcalquier has very much an air of independence and pride that makes it seem quite similar in character and attitude to towns in the Catalan flavoured areas of South West France down by the Spanish border.

The Rue de Martyrs gives pride of place to a memorial dedicated to 12 men of the town who were aged between 21 and 46 that were brutally executed on that very same street by the German occupiers, all of them died on the same day, the 8th June 1944 immediately after D-Day. This memorial serves starkly to remind you once again as do so many things here that this region of France suffered greatly not that many generations ago and it is hard to square that reality in your mind with the lively and very pleasant scenes of the modern market and the tourist throngs, most of whom do not even give the memorial a glance. It is a place to reflect.

The Monday Forcalquier market is just fabulous and you have to be very careful not to buy all the produce or at-tractive goods that catch your eye spread out on the  tempting displays. Today, we only really needed a few provisions, mainly some fish for supper from the large travelling fish van. Fish is something I abso-lutely would never buy on a Monday back home as in the UK it would be at least three days old. Also I buy an attractive useful wallet for our son James. The wallet choosing decision was a tricky one as there was a huge choice of vendors congregated all in line, mainly French Africans, who were, shall we say, rather eager for a sale. One already had our 'purchase' wrapped before I had actually decided myself. We got to an am-icable agreement in the end and he was happy at an-other sale.

We had remembered from a previous visit that there was a stall with a superb garlic display located in a tiny square just behind the main trading area of the market and we headed down the narrow ancient passageways to see if our garlic seller was still trading. Happily, large strings of garlic bulbs were hanging there and as I looked at the bewildering selection a man came up behind me and asked me if I knew about this particular garlic and its provenance. I only knew it was good garlic but I then got a very extended and detailed lecture about these fragrant bulbs with instructions on how to store it properly over the winter back in England. This expounding of enthusiastic knowledge was all totally unnecessary as I was going to buy the garlic anyway, but you will always find that the French producer loves to talk about his products.

In reality I actually didn't follow all the detail of his speech and my eyes surely glazed over but I handed over my Euros to him and had my pungent supplies that were more than sufficient for the English winter.

The funny thing is I still can't be sure it was HIS garlic.

This is a lovely peaceful square, untouched by

time and at its heart was a keyboard player sitting in the courtyard of a little café beyond the garlic stall who was playing and singing a selection of Beatles songs, of the quieter love song type. This music was the only nod to the modern era in this bucolic square. I have a friend who would have sat in this square all day long with a glass of wine or two around the ancient fountain with as many coffees as needed to stay the pace.

Just away from the square is what I consider to be one of the best little shops in France, I don't think that I exaggerate with that view, it is perfect for that something that is just a little bit different, very French of course, objects for the dining room, kitchen, bedroom. It is a delightful shop, rambling through many small rooms, not large but all so tempting. Niamh pointed out to me a beautiful glass carafe that would have been perfect for our dining room table back home. When she turned back around from telling me about it a French lady following behind her had grabbed it and headed off to pay at the till. Cheek. Sadly, these marvellous French shops never have two of the same.

Back through the narrow streets to the main market we went past a friendly café with outdoor tables that were well shaded by the high walls of the buildings and this was a tempting restaurant for lunch. We carried on shopping though and we bought a selection of buttery biscuits off a very happy biscuit seller. I sensed a young guy behind me and he asked ME how much these biscuits were being sold for and I told him despite feeling sure he was after taking my wallet. Anyway he then pushed clumsily in beyond me and paid for some and off he went. So did I with my hand closely attached to my back pocket. We tourists are definitely so cynical at times - but careful.

Further on into the market we bought some gorgeous warm crusty bread, only though after madam had finished taking extra freshly baked supplies that had just arrived from the bakery and had carefully arranged them all on the display to her precise satisfaction.

I can only but imagine that back home on a market stall in England how very quickly that would have turned to a chorus of infuriated shouts of 'can you do that later and serve us first'. Time you have to accept is not overly pressing here and you must let that be your attitude if you want to enjoy this part of Provence to the full. Be a local.

Irresistibly, our senses were compelling us to visit

the busy stall selling spit roasted chicken that sautéed the potatoes below in the dripping cooking juices as they turned slowly on the spit. This delicacy we would take back to the gite for a quiet peaceful lunch in the garden. It has to be said that chicken prepared in this way on a French market is definitely expensive compared to buying chicken back home in England but it is totally irresistible. I defy you to walk past one of these aromatic stalls on a French market and not buy. OK vegans and vegetarians excluded. Here on this stall we find that once again the concept of queuing is totally lost on the French although I suppose you cannot lose something you never had in the first place. You have a situation as you try to order at the roast chicken stall of people pushing in past you as if you don't exist to collect their pre-ordered lunch supplies and as soon as you look one way a sprightly little old lady will have somehow appeared in front of you, purse at the ready. How did she do that.

Forcalquier market was getting incredibly busy by now and we decided it was time to escape the bustling crowds. Arriving back at the parking spot we saw that our car was totally surrounded by other drivers who were searching for an elusive parking space. The only way out for us was to offer our space to a carefully selected driver and make the others aware of the futility of staying put. Fortunately, on this occasion the plan worked and eventually we managed to extricate ourselves and head home going by the same route and viewing the stupendous lavender fields and with car windows wound down the air is full of the intoxicating scent of rural Provence.

That evening Veronique says it will rain tomorrow – her computer says so.

No chance - surely not twice in a week.

Let's just say she wasn't joking.

Tuesday 19th July

The cloudy sky over the valley plain did not look too threatening when throwing back the curtains on our waking up, there were even some patches of deep blue sky interspersed between the clouds. However by nine o'clock it was raining but we could still see the village of Simiane on the hillside in the far distance. You most certainly could not see the village by half past nine though and the area of garden and patio in front of our stone cottage was seriously under very deep water. This little cloudburst was just the aperitif however and very soon the walls of the cottage were being shaken with the incredible strength of the thunder and lightning bursting around us in the fearsome sky hanging over the valley plain. The power supply to the gite was cut off and this violent storm raged on with increasing ferocity until just after eleven thirty.

At half past twelve noon we were sitting happily on the street side terrace of the restaurant Aux Fines Herbes in the small village of Goult.

In the sun, the lovely warm sun from a cloudless sky. One table on the terrace still could not be used, the rain water slowly dripping from the foliage above it but what an in-credible almost instant transformation. More importantly, what a superb lunch we were served.

We were given lovely kind service from the lady owner who patiently explained the menu so distinctly in French that she could for me have been speaking English with a Lancastrian accent. Every nuance of the dish was explained and she clearly was so totally confident that what would appear on our plate would be just as delicious as she made it sound. I would have been quite happy to have paid and left then.

Niamh had a toasted goats cheese ('ghosts toast' it appears on a menu in Bonnieux) salad rich in olive oil dressing and I had the Dourade as I so often do when choosing fish from a Provencal menu.

I am always amazed at how so many of these chefs in a small provincial restaurant can simply use so few ingredients - here in front of me is just a plate of sautéed potatoes coloured and textured to perfection, grilled Dorade and fine green beans that then leave your mouth singing with the subtle flavours developed with virgin olive oil and herbs all picked no doubt from within a short distance of the village. It is truly superb, simple, fresh and very skilful cooking.

It was a simple set panna cotta covered with a pineapple coulis that was the dessert of choice for Niamh and I enjoyed the dessert selected from the Plats du Jour chalk board. This was a brochette of fresh fruits with a warm chocolate sauce. A pichet of fruity local rosé wine had followed two Kir aperitif, one of which was made from a violet liqueur, these had complemented the meal very well as did the coffees that finished an excellent long lunch.

During our meal at the restaurant there was sat behind us a bearded middle aged man who was dining alone, being very attentive to his surroundings and every so often scribbling notes in a small, well-thumbed notepad. Playing the game like Paul Simon and Kathy on the Greyhound bus we decided that he must be a writer touring the area to source fresh ideas for his next book. At one point he got up from his table and walked behind me, and Niamh observed perhaps just a little too loudly:

'The writer's taking photos'.

He smiled, his cover blown.

The whole lunch experience had felt just as if someone had been massaging your neck and shoulders all the time during the meal. We paid the bill and moved off extremely contented and relaxed.

The village of Goult is well worth exploring and we meandered our way slowly and sleepily past the old stone houses to the summit of the hill at the top of the village topped with an old windmill and this vantage point gives some stunning panoramic views. The houses throughout Goult are individual in style, restored and well maintained, many have on their doors or gates assorted 'Beware of the Cat' signs for some reason – French sense of humour.

The village also has other restaurants that seem worthy of consideration to be your next dining venue.

The one opposite the small restaurant we had dined at was full of diners this lunchtime and had a buzzing happy atmosphere, plates being noisily cleared and wine glasses  refilled – Cafe de la Poste. The clientele here appeared to be mainly French diners which bodes well for the standard of food so although this is not by any means a Michelin starred eatery it does looks very tempting to maybe try to have lunch there on another day. Two or three other restaurants and cafes also look good and there are a couple of Butcher/Delis that draw you in. Goult is a Provencal village definitely worth a detour.

From there we went to the perched hilltop village of Gordes.

Being somewhat later in the day it was unusually easy to park the car in Gordes on this occasion. Gordes is a 'Plus Belle Village de France' and there is no denying it is spectacular and incredibly well preserved or should I say restored after the battering it took from the Nazis during the war. The views into and out of the village are breath-taking but I would never dream of buying anything from the gift shops here.

We encountered a scene inside one such over-priced shop - as this lady's resigned husband looked languidly on into the shop from a safe distance through the window outside, a 'tourist' with clearly far more money than sense purchased a clothes item at an incredibly inflated price by using the much tried and tested 'speak louder in English and they will understand' method. It all makes you want to flee the village in embarrassment.

In Gordes it is the very much the case that possibly more than anywhere else in the Luberon the tourist or more especially the American price surcharge applies. There are undoubtedly some excellent imaginative shops in the village though but most products on offer are available elsewhere at lower prices. Step inside and wander round the village and it is a version of Provence as the armchair tourist imagines it but the real Provence is not really like this at all. By all means definitely have a look at Gordes and its dramatic appearance and the great views from the village but find the real Provence elsewhere. The finest and most spectacular view is from the outside looking in.

Back at the gite I hesitatingly ask Veronique about

the weather and she says her computer has it forecast to be sunny for the rest of the week.

'Great' I say.

'But you will have the mistral' she laughed.

We English would say the weather was unsettled.

As we try to talk Ganache has cemented her jaws round my leg in that playful way of hers that somehow tends to makes any attempt at sociable conversation a little stilted, there is always that slight fear that I may not be able to persuade her to detach her jaws.

I have to say I have never ever seen her do this to Enverico.

Wednesday 20th July

For us we are finding that this week in Provence is going by extremely quickly. Today, making another early start we head up first of all to Banon to check out a potier marche we had seen advertised in the village earlier in the week. Once we are in the centre of the village there is absolutely no sign of this artisan market and when we arrived the adverts posted on the town walls earlier had disappeared. Perhaps we had misread or more likely it had been cancelled. The little village was busier than usual with people though, so maybe it was a cancellation and we were not the only disappointed ones. We decided to explore the village streets instead and headed above the village square up to the hill top through a 14th century gateway that leads on eventually to the old upper church. Many others had the same idea as we had including a high spirited group of Italian tourists walking a few paces ahead of us and clearly enjoying every moment of their stay in Provence. For them it is not an especially long journey from home and modern day Italians come in peace unlike their Roman ancestors.

What have the Romans ever done for us?

I suppose the answer in Provence is on balance – quite a lot.

The old church solidly perched on top of the hill overlooking the town had an art exhibition taking place in its interior. The French do really seem to go for the 'moderne' or unusual when it comes to holding art exhibitions. We had on a previous visit come across an exhibition in an ancient abbey organized by the resident monks that would have made anyone's Grandmothers hair curl. I have yet to come across an exhibition that shows the style we as outsiders fed on our French art in books and films would generally associate with the culture of France. I do feel having come across so much of this style of art in many exhibitions around France and particularly in the South that perhaps a retro impressionist exhibition would be a refreshing change - please.

As you get very near the top there is a beautifully restored three story house perched on the hillside set only just below the old church. It is the finest example of French shabby or Parisian chic or whatever label you wish to tag to it. It displays a sign that indicates that it belongs to an practising osteopath and we had a good laugh commenting that he must have so very few customers as you would certainly never get this far up the hillside with a bad back. The lovely house though definitely told us that it was not the case, business must be booming.

Banon village is well worth a visit either for lunch or dinner or just a ramble around its square or the characterful old town above with the expansive views over the lavender fields.

For the tourist it is ideal also for being one of the few remote villages in the Provencal countryside where you can reliably find a full range of quality supplies. You won't starve here but eat very well indeed on the local produce.

Moving on from Banon and traversing over the

plateau to Sault we drove by mile after mile of vibrant Lavender fields, the scents and smells permeating intoxicatingly into the car. This is a quite spectacular drive via the communes of St Christobel or Reveste and should under no circumstances be missed. Sault is an incredibly situated place because of the views of the Lavender fields that are enhanced by being able to gain the height to look down on to the patchwork squares of purple fields. This road towards Sault and also back to the area to the south east of Banon however are I feel probably as good as it gets for the seeker of Lavender paradise. Niamh will always require a stop to do a little 'gleaning' - with me as lookout for any emerging angry farmer.

From Sault we headed on back down from these high vantage points and followed the road to Mazan. If you have an open top sports car that needs its throttle opening up in  its rightful setting then you absolutely must head here. What a road this is. Miles of open quiet road going mainly gently downhill with panoramic views spread out before you right down to the Vaucluse as you look ahead and try to concentrate on the road. These are almost totally empty roads and you will always pass going in the other direction many brave cyclists heading up to Sault. Why do cyclists in France only seem to ride uphill? We passed one older cyclist using oxygen to enable him to go up the road on the long relentless climb to Sault.

From Mazan we drove back home after making a short stop in L'Isle sur la Sourge and made ourselves a late lunch back in the garden with bread from a local Boulanger in Apt which seemed to us to be the best bread we have ever tasted and got some eggs and milk from our enthusiastic cheese producer friend in Banon.

The shopkeeper put the six fresh eggs in a flimsy brown paper bag and handed them to us and we wondered how we would ever get those back in one piece to the gite. She just looked at our bemused faces and with a Gallic shrug of the shoulders said to be careful and so we were.

After a lazy late afternoon I cooked the wild salmon we had bought in Forcalquier and enjoyed the meal in the garden on a balmy clear evening in the fading light with another local rosé wine and slept very, very soundly.

Thursday 21st July

Ganache my resident Rottweiler friend is a very lively puppy this morning and has even been able to stir the old dog Tyson into activity as they fight over Tyson's old tyre that he is so guardedly fond of. There are many small pieces of old cuddly toys strewn around the garden and these left us in no doubt that previous young visitors have not guarded their prized possessions closely enough.

Our plan today is to partake of lunch at Le Fiacre restaurant that is situated just off the main road near to Goult but the day will not as it turns out work along with that plan. First of all we are setting out to drive over to the Abbey of Senanque that is situated just north of Gordes where there is the most moving sight of acres and acres of vivid lavender fields surrounding this ancient Cisterian abbey. Founded in 1148 the abbey was repopulated by monks as recently as 1988 and of course their main crop is lavender as well as honey, lavender honey that the region is famous for and you will find this gorgeous nectar for sale on many roadsides.

This journey though starts to develop a little bit like one of those old Peter Sellars films as we drive, or should I say try to drive towards the village of Murs and then carry out our plan to drop down to the abbey from that direction. The first 'deviation' sign we are faced with I of course just ignore as I think we can maybe get to the turn off for the abbey before the roadworks start. But no, the road is totally blocked well before that road and we have to double back to retrace our steps. Losing time we head on our route, by now obediently following the deviation signs and arrive at Murs having constantly played the usual 'can we force Les Anglais into the ditch' motoring game with the French drivers hurtling down the narrow roads. Just on the other side of the village of Murs we come across ANOTHER deviation sign that once again is a barrier to our latest preferred route down to Senanque. However, it does as a consolation take us up to a fabulous field of sunflowers and we pull the car over and join a couple of other people busily taking photos in the field. The deviation carries on down what are pretty much single track roads and it is torturous to drive through but we eventually can tell that we are on a downhill road heading towards the abbey which we can see by the distant lavender fields in the distance at the head of the valley below. As you get ever closer to Senaque Abbey there is the astonishing close up view of what looks like miles and miles of fields of lavender leading up to the abbey, the most beautiful wild flower front garden to a building imaginable. Many people have pulled up their car to the side of the road and we also decide to add to the localised congestion.

There are some camera wielding tourists that have not contented themselves with the 'official' view of the abbey and begin to dislodge the fence in front of the first field of lavender and begun to trespass right into the fields in order to gain a better shot. We you must understand behaved ourselves, being non lawbreaking English. This view is not to be missed, one of the finest in all of France. If you are within striking distance of this Abbey during the lavender season then you simply must make the effort to get here, deviation or not. The ancient abbey seems to be simply resting on a bed of lavender almost floating on this vibrant and colourful scene.

When you set the car down in the official abbey car park you then have to walk along a lavender path of about 100 metres to reach the abbey. This path is also full of visitors taking photographs. As you turn right at the end of this path you once again get a view of the abbey with more lavender set around it in an ancient walled garden.

What a breath taking location.

Some young Italians are conducting a fashion photo shoot in the courtyard garden with an antique lavender coloured bicycle as the main prop adorned of course with more fresh lavender. Unfortunately, due to our delays creating the Peter Sellers film sequel we cannot stay to spend any time looking inside the abbey and are really in any case now cutting it fine for obtaining a lunch table. We head on a route taking us back through Gordes and drop down to Le Fiacre. It is closed today. What a disappointment. We quickly turn around and head back into the village of Goult and here it seems that today there is only really the Cafe de la Poste open but it is completely bursting at the seams with happily settled diners. Clearly there is not a chance of securing a table here. There is one big difference that we have found this year and it is that most restaurants are not opening the usual long hours you would expect with this now being very much the start of high season. The lack of visitors this summer is strikingly obvious, with virtually no English tourists to be seen, very few Americans and even less Japanese. The main visitors are clearly the Belgians and the Dutch along with quite a few Germans, all EU citizens on the same land mass. Those tourists that normally have a sea to cross are surely feeling the effects of the economic climate at this time and staying away from France with a consequent detrimental effect on the restaurants.

Our very last chance at what is becoming a late hour to be enjoying lunch has to be in Bonnieux and the restaurant St Andre though we found it only 'OK' last year despite having used it many times before on our visits and usually loved it. They do serve lunch later here so it had to be worth a try.

The village of Bonnioux itself was fairly busy but we did get a table at St Andre. It was refreshingly clear that the restaurant has had a refurbishment facelift since our last visit and was trying to upgrade a level in quality. There is for the table new cutlery and plates and a much changed fresh décor was also in evidence throughout. Sadly, wine served by the carafe was no longer available and you feared that perhaps the food may have been changed a little too much also.

The food had indeed changed from last year and it has to be said it was a change very much for the better. The fresh ingredients were local and of high quality and very well pre-  pared and presented. Niamh had as is her custom for lunch on a hot Provencal summer's day a goats cheese salad that was large and fresh and I had an Entrecote steak and frites. The meat was tender and succulent, looking only just slightly more cooked than a piece you would buy fresh from the butchers display and I was well satisfied. More attention to detail had gone into the range of desserts also – I had an assiette of Normandy apple tart, Chantilly cream, ice cream and an expresso coffee, Niamh a beautiful fruit tart that was a simply a picture on the plate. Wine was local and excellent and we were very happy.

This was a vast improvement on last year although the service despite being efficient and prompt could have had a touch more interest and love put into it. It was a bit perfunctory. The trip advisor sign said put a review on so I think a 4 out of 5, a tweak of the service quality and perhaps a five the quality and cooking of the food actually deserved.

The terrace of St Andre is a good place to people watch - either those seated on this terrace or people meandering along the street winding down from the top of the village. At one point during the meal an elderly American couple came in, both were aged around 80 or more and Niamh and I remarked that it was great to see people of that age having the courage to travel so far and still clearly revelling in the experiences. After they had finished the main part of the meal they just ordered one apple tart and two spoons between them for their dessert and the husband took pictures of it from every possible angle and they certainly entertained the diners. I have started to have a tendency to photograph our meals when dining out to use for reference back home in the kitchen and we both though that this could be a picture of us in a few years' time.

We left the restaurant and rather than attempting a climb up to the church we turned left down one of the many narrow winding lanes that lead to the lower town. Just below the restaurant there was a small ancient stone seat that looked out over the Luberon plain so we were happy to crash out there for a while taking in the sun and the wonderful views of the Luberon as we heard above and below us the village starting to come to life again after everyone's lunch has been enjoyed.

For the evening we did not really want much more in the way of food so we deliberated in the garden with little success as to what to have to eat until the time had got to about 8 o'clock when Veronique came outside with two individual wild cherry clafoutis just for us. This was just what was needed and so very kind of her as they were busy preparing food for supplying to a wedding reception the next day and all day they had been and still were working very hard. This is a most relaxing hospitable place.

One thing that we have enjoyed about the cottage and the location has been the variety of wildlife (although not ALL of it.).

We spent part of the evening watching the resident eagle in the lavender field behind the cottage waiting patiently for it to go into flight but it refused and stayed perched on the wooden fence post until we gave up hoping. The garden is teeming with butterflies but especially dragon/damselflies. An owl made a welcome appearance in the trees in the garden and we could hear its pleasant sound long into the night. The strangest noise we have heard this week in the garden has definitely been from inside the tree canopies themselves.

Frogs! Definitely lots and lots of frogs. We have never seen one in the shallow wildlife pond but we have certainly heard them.

I said to Veronique ' I know this is a stupid question but are there frogs in your trees?'

'Mais oui! Certainement.'

'Not usually in England' I said.

Perhaps it was the wine talking.

Friday July 22nd

Sadly, this is our last day here - surely not. It has all gone so very quickly. We don't actually feel that we have done as many touristy things or travelled around the region quite as much as the last time that we were in the area but what we have certainly benefited from on our trip this year is a great sense that we have totally wound down mentally and physically and the realisation that we badly needed to do that. It had to be faced that we will be back in the real world quite soon enough. On we will go to Grasse and the French Riviera region tomorrow and I think we are ready to engage a bit more closely with France and its people now that we are relaxed and refreshed. This gentle quiet area of Provence has worked her magic on us.

Today the main event is that we simply have to get our promised lunch at Le Fiacre restaurant close to Goult. On the way over we pay a visit to the Cave Sylla in Apt which has a tempting variety of their wines on offer and a generous well laid out tasting area. They also have a section of the building that is laid out as a restaurant with a set menu of an assiette of local goodies with wines paired by the glass to compliment them. Our plans are firmly set for lunch however and the wine area in the cave is busy so we head off to the restaurant determined to be early.

When we arrive at La Fiacre two tables on the outside terrace are already occupied and we are actually given the same table that we dined at on our previous visit.

It is as last time a friendly welcome and also just as occurred previously the amuse bouches are provided immediately and then a second pre-starter plate of goat cheese toasts followed by some anchovies wrapped in puff pastry alongside two types of olives.

A great start to lunch with chilled bubbly kir royals as an aperitif.

Niamh chose the chicken terrine with salad as her starter and I had a stack of tomato and smoked salmon with a salad. Both were absolutely delicious and very fresh produce.

After that we both could not resist a chunky fillet of pan fried sea bass with a tomato sauce with those vegetables cut the way the French love in long strips, no doubt with one of those gadgets sold on the market. Why do we in England just get very thin sea bass fillets, and where do the French source these monsters? There were carrots and two types of courgette and artichokes (not in strips).The other accompaniment was barley slow cooked with herbs and peppers.

The whole plate just was so fresh and perfectly balanced – a real treat.

After that Niamh had melon and sorbet drenched in Beaumes de Venice and I had crème caramel with red berries.

Coffee and more nibbles of meringue and tuiles completed a long and really memorable lunch.

We really had thought long and hard about coming here again as the last time we had lunch here it was just so perfect and to have come again and then found that we were disappointed perhaps by a new chef or new owners or just a drop in standards would have spoilt any previous memory of the place. We were very pleased to find that if anything the whole experience was even better this time and you could see that hard work had gone into trying to make the dishes even more attractive and flavoursome. What an end to this leg of the trip. There most definitely was a feeling of wellbeing leaning back in my chair on this gorgeous warm afternoon.

Arriving back In Goult we waited in the sun contentedly by the village square for the deli that is part of the local butchers shop to re-open again after they had finished their long lunch. Eventually they opened rather sleepily at around 3.30 and the friendly owners greeted us and we choose some pates and tapenades to take home from his lovely selection.

Back at La Buissonade we simply chilled out in the garden. Veronoque and Enverico had another delivery to do in the van and I had been playing with Ganache. As they came out of their little 'factory' Ganache ran over to them and then realized they were packing the van to go out on deliveries.

Like a young child she quickly turned and ran back to us and settled by our chairs, cleverly, she thought, showing that it would be OK to leave her with us and she could stay  out and continue to play. Veronique put paid to her hopes and she had to go inside the house.

Sad dog

Saturday 23rd July

It is our day for travelling on by taking the Auto-Route farther south and east to the Riviera to start an extra stay in Provence near to the perfume town of Grasse. We were very sad that we had now to leave La Buissonade and before departing Veronique kindly gave us a bottle of local red wine to take home. Sad, because it is most likely that we will not return to stay at La Buissonade in the future as there are so many places in France and Provence that you would like to experience. However, you never know for we have grown extremely fond of this little 'family' and I think the feelings are mutual. I think, yes I think there were very nearly tears.

We arrived at our Bed and Breakfast stay of La Surprise located slightly north east of Grasse by 1 o'clock after having had a little difficulty finding the place. If you ever have the urgent need to be somewhere totally incognito and never ever to be found then this house should be high on your list as an option although the house is in actual fact very close to the main road coming out of Grasse.

We were quickly and warmly welcomed with a chilled glass of rosé by Clare and Steve and the old house looked stunningly beautiful with fabulous views from the poolside looking down on the amphitheatre spread out before you stretching to the sea at Nice.

You could just sit and watch the planes coming in over the sea to land at Nice Airport. Steve gave us the very welcome option of using the summer kitchen and barbeque and we thought that we might just do that on what was sure to be a balmy evening. The room we had booked was beautifully and tastefully decorated and furnished with a superb bathroom, all had been carefully thought out and accomplished to a very high standard of quality and finish.

After chatting for a while to our hosts and gaining a couple of local suggestions and also after browsing the extensive 'guide book' expert. prepared by them we headed to the village of Valbonne. This is an old town built on a cross grid system reminding you of a picturesque small version of Milton Keynes, only the grid system here seemed to make sense.It was very interesting and productive to explore up and down the narrow streets looking at the shops and artists as well as spending time chilling out in the atmospheric main square which is completely enclosed by tempting restaurants. This certainly was a very appealing location to stop for a while and have a glass of rosé or stay on into the evening to eat.

There were restaurants not only in the square but there were also quite a selection leading off down the adjacent grid that also looked inviting but we decided to go and buy some  fresh fish and vegetables for the barbecue and use that for tonight's meal.

If you decide to visit Valbonne then this square may seem a little familiar to you. Some scenes of the film 'French Kiss' starring Meg Ryan were filmed here and the attractive square was the venue for the fight scene between the two brothers.

It is a village that has been sympathetically brought into the 21st century and the planners have retained most of its medieval provincial French character. This charming village is an excellent one for us to find so close to our accommodation.

After our all too brief visit to Valbonne we drove our car far up into the hills ending up at the village of Gourdon, a settlement that somehow clings to the hillside some 940 metres up from sea level and Nice appearing as if a miniature village spread across the bay below.

How spectacular is this.

The drive up the typic-ally winding Riviera road is in itself something special but when you eventu-ally snake your way  around the curves of the pass to get to the very top the views are simply breath-taking as you look way down over the Riviera – a scene spanning from Nice to well past Cannes and even viewing as far as the island of Corsica in the very far distance.

The villages and towns set below are presented to your eyes as being so small and vertically below that you could easily imagine that you were viewing them from a seat in a plane. The mountains wrap around the whole panoramic scene from behind you and I can honestly say it is one of the most impressive viewpoints I have ever had the pleasure of finding myself in.

This small village of Gourdon has a very relaxed feel to it despite its prime reason for existence seemingly being to serve the tourist trade these days, including us of course. We bought a few small presents for home from one of the many perfume shops, being served by a very happy assistant who danced and sang as she wrapped. Don't get that in Tesco's.

Near the edge of this perched viewpoint there is inevitably yet another perfume shop and Niamh got seriously detained by the very persistent lady standing guard outside this boutique. Madam was most disdainful when we eventually managed to convince her that we had no intention of buying. She could not understand why we would not readily consent to letting her douse us with her vast array of fragrant samples. One thing we have quickly come to realise about the region around the perfume capital of Grasse is there are inevitable consequences for you if you let yourself be charmed in any of the many fragrance shops because once outside your newly acquired scented aroma will make you a sitting duck for all the insects in the area.

We sat and enjoyed looking over the edge of the viewpoint and all that was spread out beneath us and cooled down with a very rich ice cream as we took in the sights again. I think for sure that this village will be a return trip for us back up the mountainside in the next day or so.

Just on the edge of the village as you are returning to the car park there is located a house set below the level of the road which has a long allotment type garden where the owner is growing vegetables and salads in the most fabulous of settings. If you are self-catering in the area for a few days it is really worth a look around. Produce couldn't be fresher.

Retracing our steps carefully back down the mountainside and trying to keep my eyes on the road and not the view, we eventually arrived back at La Surprise and we fired up the BBQ for which Steve has kindly prepared the coals and wood and soon I had some tomatoes, peppers and fish sizzling away. The other two couples that are staying at La Surprise made an appearance by the pool, Ed and Vanessa (Dutch and Spanish) and Oscar and Francesco (both Italian). Meeting them turned into a very pleasant evening in their lovely engaging company.

Ed and Vanessa intention was to be going out quite late in to Cannes but Vanessa said:

'Why go when we are enjoying the company here'.

The food was shared and eaten and the available wine was finished and everyone went to bed very happy with an evening spent together and once again new friendships were made.

Sunday 24th July

For our Sunday in the area we decided that after a copious breakfast of fresh fruit, croissants, pastries, bread and jams provided by Clare that we would head up to St Paul de Vence. I have to say that I was a bit apprehensive about this decision with it being Sunday as we thought St Paul may turn out to be very busy. As you approach St Paul you become very aware of the many 'real estate' agents (not mere Estate agents here.) that are situated on the approach to the village. The money that has and still is spilling into the area is obvious for all to see.

It was a short stroll from parking our car down to the entrance into the village. Around a café there was a large boule space that had some highly competitive games taking place between the locals. The wine was already flowing and shouts of delight or frustration coming from the players. A very French scene.

St Paul as it turned out was actually not too busy at all and we strolled comfortably around the very narrow streets. The first winding lane you come to is well populated by artist  studios and you really must make a determined effort to never catch their eye or your credit card is in for a pounding. No prices at all are displayed here and I would suggest that it is best not to ask or show an interest. There is undoubtedly some fine art here if perhaps a touch vibrant for an English dining room wall in winter. I always feel certain that unpriced art is out of my price range however and I am reluctant to test that theory. The streets ramble on ever upwards and you eventually find your way to the church at the top of the village and again excellent panoramic views are to be had as you wind your way around the church over to the village ramparts.

We took a route down a narrow lane passing behind the church and away from any shops and in a quiet passageway we came across a small boy who was playing alone quite boisterously. As we got closer to him he made his move and strangely tried to take me prisoner in his weird game and was determined that he would not let me go. Eventually I wrestled my arms free from this crazy child and headed back up to the church very much to Niamh's amusement. We carried on safely and went past many fine shops and artisans but once again they are exceptionally overpriced despite undoubted quality.

It is all there for you to look and admire but buy elsewhere with tourist premium deducted from the inflated prices. In the lane to the left leading from the entrance gate there was a talented accordion player performing for the early diners that were sat at the tables that spilled  out on to street and it was an especially pleasant and a very French lunchtime scene. It certainly was extremely hot by now and we managed to find some shelter away from the blazing sun and be seated close to a street stall that was selling panninis and salads, cold drinks etc and decided to purchase a snack from there for our lunch.

At around 2 o'clock we decided to move on from Saint Paul and headed back down towards the Mediterranean coast. The city of Nice was clearly busy today – well, that is, I thought it was busy as I couldn't find a way in or anywhere to park and taking advantage of Niamh being asleep in the car I quietly moved down the coast road towards Antibes. We eventually contented ourselves with just a look at the Mediterranean and travelled on inland to Mougins despite the best efforts of the French road system planners to disguise where it was.

Mougins is an extremely beautiful small village that is famous for its residents culinary exploits, in a similar way to say Padstow in England, home to Rick Stein and other high profile chefs. There are some lovely restaurants surrounding the small square around its old fountain and these are complemented by a high end restaurant sited there also. Roger Verge has two fine restaurants located just off the main square. Along with Verge, Alain Ducasse has an association with the restaurant L'Amandier. Mougins due to its long standing culinary heritage is also home to a Gastronomic festival each year in September.

The sister restaurant of the two associated with Verge is quite reasonably priced and we thought we would have a look at possibly eating at that one tomorrow but we in any case  would definitely return to the delightful Mougins for lunch - a long one.

The narrow car free streets are extremely pleasant and interesting with many artists and artisans having studios here. The 91 year old Picasso died here in Mougins in 1973 having lived out the last 12 years of his life in the village. There is a fine museum of art in the village that is not to be missed. There are at least three tempting shops for items, essential or otherwise for the home and dining table as well as the exceptional Deli attached to Verges restaurant that also sells a small range of kitchen and table ware.

To quietly sit around the village fountain and listen contentedly to the quiet hum of the restaurants now serving afternoon drinks on their terraces is an extremely enjoyable interlude. Mougins is a perfect little place and we decide that we will indeed come back tomorrow.

So off we go back to La Surprise and it was an easy decision to have another BBQ, Steve had very kindly cleaned and prepared it for us once again and tonight we were joined mainly by Oscar as Ed and Vanessa finally did go out for that trip into Cannes later. Oscar was at a loose end as his girlfriend had a headache and stayed in her room and so we talked and ate and drank long into the evening and had the most pleasant end to a very agreeable day.

Oscar was very easy company and clearly enjoys meeting people and talking about an interesting range of subjects and we have enjoyed his delightful company very much indeed.

Monday 25th July

After an early breakfast on the terrace looking down to the sea at Nice and saying goodbye to Ed and Vanessa who are taking the long drive home via what Ed and I agree will be an expensive little shopping detour to Italy we drove for our first visit the short distance in to Grasse itself. We parked easily in the underground car park close by the bandstand and the many perfume houses and so were well positioned to start to explore the town. Our first port of call was at the Perfume museum associated with Fragonard. It has to be said that I thought this museum may not be exactly my cup of tea but the visit and tour of the museum did in fact turn out to be just as interesting for me as it was for Niamh. She really enjoyed seeing the fascinating displays, particularly a fairly extensive and I would imagine reasonably priceless collection of old vinaigrettes, perfume holders and bottles. This is a really excellent and free museum that has to be well worth a slice of your time when you are in Grasse.

The narrow streets of the old town begin just near this museum and Grasse turns out to be quite different to any other town we have visited on this Provencal leg of the trip.

There is clearly in evidence a large North African population living and working here and the old town has a feel to it that is somewhat similar to Perpignan, a little edgy no doubt in the evening. Around every corner of these narrow lanes there is a discovery, perhaps a small square or another narrow high sided street or even a dead end. Grasse seems to revel in the somewhat faded character that adorns a lot of the buildings in the old town but these only add to its charm and interest, a great place for a keen photographer to wander and explore – the photo opportunities to be found here in the old town are endless. We loved it and walked on up to the church and the square beyond. From the walls on the edge of the square the viewpoint gives, as seems to be always the case in this region the most fabulous panorama.

Then sitting quietly in the square and just when you thought you had seen everything in France, Grasse and Provence surprises you again. This charming square was decked out (sorry.) with brightly coloured deck chairs and overhead you could see and hear what appeared to be steam hissing from small pipes attached to the old grand houses encircling the square. However, this is not steam, no, Grasse is the perfume centre of France, so it turned out to be a perfumed steam spray and it filled the entire square with its fragrance and gave off what we assume was intended to be a relaxing feel to the square as you sat there in a comfortable deck chair. I just cannot see it catching on in England but as an advertising ploy for the town's main reason for being it was very effective - how could you not be drawn into one of its many fragrance shops now?

We would really have liked to have stayed longer in Grasse but we especially wanted to go back to the village of Mougins for lunch and we wandered back to the car park by another route through another bustling square housing many restaurants of varying character and already having incoming diners but unfortunately not quite tempting enough to make us decide to stay.

A Diversion – The incident with the French Pod Toilet

There are moments in life when something occurs that is just so funny that it transcends the acute discomfort of the participants. Or am I just describing the warped English sense of humour. Probably.

I am not sure, well actually I am totally sure, if Niamh even now years later finds this story amusing. Just before leaving Grass it was once again a case of hunt the loo, a game that is played out extensively all over France. We eventually found one; you know the ones, that peculiarly French invention of the enclosed toilet pods with curved sliding door – 50 cents a go.

I left Niamh in a short queue at this one, a particularly fine example, complete with correct coinage and wandered off towards the church to take some more photographs and also to take in the old faded architecture of the large square.

Suddenly my peace and concentration is shattered by a Frenchman shouting rather excitedly :

'Monsieur, monsieur. Votre femme, votre femme'.

It was obvious it was to me that he was directing his frantic words and wanted me to hurry along with him and all the while he is turning back at me and pointing in the direction of the pod toilet.

I arrived quickly and Niamh was standing outside the said pod, very, very wet indeed. I had thought it was a loo not a power shower cubicle and she was being dried off by the waiting queue of bemused people. She was not happy to say the least.

What had happened here, although I suspect you may have guessed the scenario by now, was that a German tourist was in the queue immediately before her and kindly, in retrospect I use the word advisedly, held the door open so that she could go in after her for free.

The swivel door had closed behind Niamh as normal but because of the pod brain not having been fed 50 cents it then thought that the pod was now empty and had decided it was time to go into a full cleaning mode with the added feature of turning off the lights with Niamh trapped inside.

She screamed to no avail but somehow she did manage to find the exit button and get out of the pod but not before the damage was most certainly done.

I remember many years ago watching an episode of the finest British comedy Fawlty Towers (Google if confused), the one where Basil tries to move the body of the deceased hotel guest from his room before he gets slated on Trip Advisor. It was and still is hysterically funny but at the time my mother did not think it in particularly good taste and sat there watching stony faced and expected us to do the same. I somehow managed to do that but probably caused irreparable lasting damage to my insides. This situation here in Grasse was one such moment, I could not laugh but had to sympathise and find a means of drying her out assuming that sometime later we could have a very good laugh about it.

I am still waiting.

To Continue:

It was an extremely hot (clothes drying) midday sun when we arrived in Mougins and we strolled slowly up into the old village and after a short consideration of restaurant options we eventually decided on Le Rendevous de Mougins Restaurant in the village square. It had a lovely shaded terrace that reminded you of good times past, you could imagine Monet or Gauguin sat there over a long lunch. In any case the terraces of the other restaurants were a little more located in the direct sunlight. The lunchtime menu looked good and the place was very busy, seemingly not just with tourists and that balance of clientele suits me fine.

After enjoying our aperitif of cool Kirs we both choose the Fish terrine to start the meal and then Niamh had Salmon with a good selection of accompaniments and I had the 4 cheese ravioli with pesto and tomato sauce. We both had panna cotta to finish and these were served unusually in Kilner jars.

This was a really good lunch and excellent fixed price value. As we are so close to the Italian border it is very much a restaurant with an Italian twist about the cooking but all was well done and flavoursome. Not high end stuff but just good honest fresh cooking by a talented chef using the freshest of local ingredients. My kind of place.

The service unusually for restaurants in France was very efficient in the speedy sense of the word and we had to actually slow it down ourselves otherwise our meal could even have felt slightly rushed which is most certainly not the norm in France.

We wandered happily over to the fountain in the square and sat next to it for a while in the welcoming shade and absorbing the gentle sound of the splashing water. However it was not long before our peace was disturbed by groups of young local schoolchildren on some sort of treasure hunt with their teachers. French schoolchildren out in public are so well behaved and at one point a small group of young girls detached themselves from the others and came rushing up to us and very politely asked if we knew of a particular location that they needed to find next.

Of course I am afraid that we didn't know but they all thanked us anyway and said goodbye.

Later another group of them had suddenly found a location located on their map and Niamh was stood right in the firing line of this onrushing group and ended up surrounded by them as they made their way excitedly past her. It was a very funny tableau and the teachers were having a good chuckle at the scene of the cornered 'Anglais'.

At least she did not get pushed into the fountain.

Back on our tour of the village streets we bought some items to adorn our dining table back home from two of the lovely shops. In the second I was complimented on my French speaking which is always welcome as you feel on some days that you are not doing that well with the language.

After taking another little siesta, having made sure that the children had finished their hunt for the day, we headed off up the winding mountain road to Gourdon again and arrived in that high perched village. We really have enjoyed coming up to this village once more to be able to have a good stroll, and we have the village more to ourselves today, taking in the views again and buying a couple of fairly 'clichéd' Provencal gifts for some friends. Well you have to don't you?

Back at La Surprise we BBQ'd again that evening after going back to the local supermarket for supplies. Our shopping expedition was on this occasion a traumatic experience to say the least. Turning off the left hand exit from the roundabout towards the super-market I accelerated away (as you do) looked up and found another car coming straight towards me. We both swerved and I could see the startled driver being fiercely berated by an old woman in the passenger seat, a lady that I assume was his mother. Not sure if she was beating him over the head with an umbrella as they do in films but she was not happy. A French-man on the wrong side of the road – how did he get there? A real 'life flashed before us moment'.

Finally in the supermarket (eventually and shakily) we were stood pondering the extensive rosé wine selection and I could sense that a man who was doing his own shopping was observing us. He then came over and started to inform us all about the char-acter of some of these wines and which ones were his particular favourites and why he liked them. By the end of his lecture he had upgraded our intended pur-chase in monetary value quite substantially – and he was only a customer. Not used to that in Tesco's. Now that was genuine 'customer' service. We thanked him and headed back to La Surprise. Just as he had prom-ised the selected wine was by the way – excellent.

It was a lovely last evening, very mild, still and peaceful. The garden and pool area of La Surprise is most attractive and a great place to chill in an evening. The sky was clear and a multitude of stars filled the heavens and down below we had the panorama leading round to the bright lights of Nice and the scattered lights of the hillside houses dotted around this amphitheatre. A great finale to a very enjoyable stay.

The next morning it was a case of early goodbyes to Steve and Clare and Oscar and Francesca after yet another superb breakfast provided by Clare. What a super place and I recommend it unreservedly. Well there is just one reservation; here you must not bring anything too big car wise. You may never get it back out again as the name La Surprise is purely because it is a great surprise to eventually find it and an even greater surprise that you have remembered your three point turn skills to get out again.

A Journey home

After a couple of weeks touring Provence it can feel a little flat to just go straight back home to England so we would usually make a short stop for a couple of days, more often than not in Burgundy. I hope this short conclusion to our story of Provence can inspire you to add another region to your travels and turn the travelling itself into part of the French holiday experience. If you are heading home to America from Paris this also is a fine way to end a trip to France rather than heading straight to the airport.

On this occasion we had a short stop in Beaune before spending a couple of days in Vezaley, an historical town in Northern Burgundy and a place full of interest and possibilities. This was a new place for us to explore and a fitting end to a fantastic two weeks in Provence.

The actual journey from Beaune we wanted to turn into a full day of interest rather than it purely being a travelling day so we decided to head across country to the hilltop wine village of Sancerre.

We especially wanted to have lunch at the Joseph Mellot Auberge located in the village square where we have dined before and really to see once again a town that we are very fond of as it had been about six years since our last visit. It is also home to Niamh's favourite wine – white Sancerre.

Arriving in Sancerre we found that it was quite busy especially compared to what we had experienced overnight in Beaune so we quickly sat at the

solitary available table at the Auberge. We noticed that madam who runs the front of house and on past visits over the last ten years was very lively and totally in bustling command had with age slowed down a little now and she was a touch calmer but she was still the one that took all the orders before allowing the waitress to get involved. I can't imagine her wanting to give up her role as commander in chief just yet.

As expected the food was excellent and I had that tasty Burgundy speciality Oeufs en Meurette and then a rare steak and Niamh had Chavignol Goats cheese salad (as usual) and then a Cocotte of fish in a rich creamy sauce. Chavignol is a small pretty village a short distance from Sancerre that is famous for its small round goats cheeses and also make high quality wine that carries the Sancerre appellation.

We were very amused when an elderly lady started to make her way around the tables displaying for all to see her dessert. She was ecstatic about this gorgeous dish of pears cooked in Sancerre red wine and wanted all to see the dish that had made her day. I was pleased about that as I had just ordered the same finale to my meal. The waitress came over to the man sat with his wife at the next table and he ordered the pears – how could he resist. Sadly, he was informed that I had ordered the last one. I could not resist a slight self-satisfied smirk on my face. It was like winning the lottery.

All this superb meal was of course accompanied by a Mellot Sancerre from their own vineyard. Worth the trip.

We had intended to buy some wine in Sancerre but the current prices are to be honest little different to buying the bottles in the UK so not much point carrying it back really so we decided to leave purchasing this time round. Sancerre is a very pleasant village to stroll around and some new shops have appeared since our last visit as well as some familiar ones having closed. We have found that over the last couple of visits that in Burgundy and the Loire Valley there has been quite a renewal of the type and quality of shops in the region and mainly this change has been for the better.

One small artisan shop that had closed in Sancerre was a pottery where we had bought a beautiful piece from the lady artisan some years ago – a sign on the door simply said:

'It was time to give my time to the children'. Lovely sentiments but for her customers it was a shame nonetheless as there was some fine talent there.

We strolled off the main square and down the narrow streets opposite the Auberge and came to another smaller square in front of the Marie or Town Hall. It was market day in Sancerre. However this market was the smallest one in France, just one stall selling a good range of fruit and vegetables and they had an orderly queue of faithful followers. Quite an odd sight to see as we are used to markets in France being packed with traders and full of crowds of people.

Leading out from the Marie square there was one of the new shops and this was an artisan handbag maker whose range was quite stunning. As we had not bought any wine to fill the car then a hand bag for Niamh's next Paris trip (soon) seemed to be a better value purchase and as we received the usual pleasant and enthusiastic service that we have come to expect in shops like this in France then Niamh was soon convinced it was an excellent idea and the choice was made.

We had a brief rest on a bench by the walls overlooking the valley below the village from the high vantage point that is offered from Sancerre. This is a stunning panorama that is set out before you and you can pick out the features of the landscape and it all looks like a view in miniature such is your commanding position. Happy with our detour we took ourselves off to Vézelay.

Arriving in Vézelay we found our hotel which was the Hotel Compostelle located at the foot of the town and were greeted very cheerfully by the lady on reception and settled in to our quite basic but clean and comfortable room. The room may be basic but what a view it offers from the rear of the hotel looking down over the valley and at this time of year you are blessed with vast fields of sunflowers. There is tonight an added bonus of the most fabulous sunset over the valley and it seems we have made a very good choice of hotel.

Tonight, after that long and substantial lunch in Sancerre we did not require any more food so we strolled on the upward path towards the Basilica that dominates the town, a route that has no doubt been taken by thousands of pilgrims over the centuries, taking our time to look around Vézelay. This was a lovely pleasant time to do it as the coaches of the many day tourists had gone and all was calm.

Vézelay appears to be another town that has had quite a facelift with seemingly many new shops, some of them quite boutique in style and this is reflected in the prices and the whole town looks freshly scrubbed and revived. We sat for a time near the Cathedral and it was very peaceful on a warm and still evening with just the occasional soft peel of the bells. All was well with the world.

We took the opportunity to check out the restaurant possibilities for our stay (not tonight though – tummies too full). One looked particularly promising but as we sat near it the chef and his commis chef came out for a cigarette break.

Let's just say that on that appearance they were never going to be cooking anything for us – the restaurant was full later and I do hope all the diners are alright tomorrow.

A couple of restaurants are now on the list so we shall see what we decide.

It has been a long day but worth the effort to in effect give ourselves an extra day by taking in Sancerre.

The weather in the morning is grey and a bit miserable and we head off after a good breakfast at the hotel to spend a little time in nearby Clamecy and park the car by the port where the canal meets the Yonne River. The streets wind up steeply to the large church, an old building that is very run down in appearance and in much need of some renovation. The square is unusual in having a variety of some timeworn buildings that are now trading as shops running in a line from the side of the church door giving a complete lack of symmetry to the frontage of the ancient church. Across from the shops is a massive Marie, well out of proportion to the size of the town of Clamecy and this again has seen better days. In fact the town as a whole gives off an air of neglect which is surprising given its proximity to Vézelay and the tourism that should come in to here from the canal and river. We wandered back to the port by another route passing the town war memorial - unusually this memorial has been left in a destroyed state after the Nazis desecrated it in the occupation. It does make quite an effective statement though.

We watched for a while as some boats made their way through the locks and this part of Clamecy made for a pleasant scene to relax in for a while.

When you are sat by the canal, life on it always looks like something you really want to experience one day until you see the rigmarole involved every time these boats get to a lock. Still firmly in the pending tray is this type of holiday.

The decision was made to head to Chablis, another favourite wine town of ours and as we went across country through some small but fairly prosperous wine villages such as Irancy the weather started to deteriorate. As we could see Auxerre in the distance bathed in sunshine I decided to turn the car and head over there. The riverside town of Auxerre has provided quite a range of experiences for us on many past visits, mainly good ones. We have very good memories of some truly superb meals at Maximes, Le Jardin Gourmand or Le Salamader. However Auxerre does have a faded feel to it but I find that is not totally unattractive.

Again as with Vezaley, Auxerre also appears to be in the midst of a facelift particularly as regards the old Cathedral that looked on the verge of falling down on our last visit about five years previously. Most of our previous visits to Auxerre have been for specific wine tours and I will write about wine as a separate subject in another book.

We bought some snacks from a boulangere and had a pleasant picnic lunch by the river watching the boats go by and observing some others mooring up by the riverside in front of Maximes.

Thankfully, the weather was improving slightly

as we headed back to Vezaley and it was pleasant to have a beer and coffee on a terrace near the Basilica. There was a garden that was open to the public just off the square in front of the Basilica that had belonged to the French writer Jules Roy who from a brief look around the house seemed to have had a very interesting life to say the least. The garden was very attractive with great views down the valley but the main feature of this space was a bizarre sculpture exhibition consisting of about 50 or so individual but similar pieces strung through the terrace, each piece filled with shells. Apparently it was a dragon. I can only feel he was a friend of Dali. Interesting.

Again something that has been a feature of our time here in Burgundy is that choices are limited for dinner because of restaurant holiday closures. I know I really shouldn't be surprised but I find it strange that a greater effort is not made to take advantage of a large captive audience at this peak time for foreign travellers – why not take the money and have your holiday later in the year? It is a quirk of French culture but I suppose you could say the old Lancashire Wakes weeks in England are just the same principle.

We decided not to take any expensive risks and ate at La Coquille as that restaurant has always seemed busy and on the previous night when looking in everybody seemed to be having a good time. This was probably our one mistake so far on this trip and one of the few dining disappointments we have had in France. The starters were fine and the desserts again quite acceptable but the mains were awful.

I had an impenetrable entrecote steak and Niamh allegedly a very dry piece of sea bass. Sea Bass - I don't think so! I only didn't complain because they might have brought another and I already knew that what I had eaten already would stay with me, mentally and physically for some time. We also had to order the wine three times and only got that quite some time after the main course arrived. Service was of the throw it at you variety with clearly too few staff. One to avoid.

An early morning visit to the Basilica is recommended and with very few people around it is a good time to take in the astonishing structure - as the French are heard to say continually - 'incroyable' architecture. It really is difficult, no actually impossible to get your head round how they managed to build such a technically difficult and immense structure all those many centuries ago. I said to Niamh that you could just imagine on build 'day one' someone laying one of the large stones at the base and saying: 'Come on men - soon get this finished'.

It is an incredible feat.

Historically Vezeley is one of the most important religious sites in France and back in the time of the inception of the Basilica it was perhaps the foremost site of faith in the country. Vézelay in fact was chosen as the venue for the preaching of the second crusade in 1146 but rather fell out of favour after a certain increase in scepticism of the provenance regarding the relics held in the Basilica.

The interior makes excellent use of the available light and has quite a sense of space and light and appears from its condition to have been built recently rather than the 1100's. Except in the crypt that is and Niamh wouldn't go down there. The square in front of the large front  doors is a very quiet and peaceful place to sit before or after the tourists take over the village. Vezaley is very much a village with two faces and to be there early and later in the day is a big contrast to the day-time when coachloads of tourists park at the base of the village and wind their way up in pilgrimage to the Basilica.

One time on the way up we were engaged in conversation by a lady owner of a small wine outlet representing a viniculteur just outside the village and we promised to return later – 8.30 is too early even for us for a wine tasting.

Also on the way up to the basilica was a window displaying pottery from an artisan in St Pere a small village located below Vézelay and later in the morning we headed over to St Pere to have a look. Going inside her artisan studio we could not see anything at all on display, just the potter working in a cramped mezzanine with all the clay and tools scattered randomly around the room. She took us down a rickety staircase and it was there that she had a well set out display in the cellar, in and out of which her cat was walking perilously close to the fairly expensive pieces. We liked what we saw and bought a green jug and small pot that would go well with our other decorations back home, said our goodbyes and headed on as we wanted to explore as much as we could of the local area today. St Pere also has a fairly large church for the size of village and also an even older one that was burned down many centuries ago in some religious wars and the interior was then used as a graveyard within the ruined walls. Very strange and not a place to have a picnic in at night I think.

We went on via the D100 to Chatel-Censoir where in the square there was a small market in full swing. The roast chicken on the spit was very tempting for lunch but we resisted and wandered down to the quiet canal side and surprisingly came across a man selling wine and offering wine tasting from a small tent. It reminded me of some of those sketches on Monty Python where the most unexpected thing is for no apparent reason placed in a familiar mundane setting.

He was very friendly and quickly without much resistance from ourselves led us into trying a few whites especially a Saint Bris, Coteaux d'Auxerre and a Luginy Macon, all very fine and we bought a mixed case from him.

He had observed Niamh looking at some corkscrews that he had on display but we thought them a little light in construction, we had actually wanted to buy a good new one and looked at many examples this week particularly in the exclusive wine establishments in Beaune but price wise they were very expensive there. He then smiled, broke off from packing our case of wine and said he had a 'petit cadeaux' for Niamh and produced a really lovely corkscrew, with wooden inlay, sat in a wallet and boxed up. This was extraordinarily kind as it was just the quality we had been looking at in Beaune and usually at a retail price of between 30 or 40 euros. We left very pleased indeed with an excellent tasting, good wine purchases and a remarkably generous gift. This corkscrew I still use (almost every day), a favourite possession.

We went back to Vézelay for lunch and ate on the terrace of our hotel where they had put on a basic small lunchtime menu and it was extremely pleasant sitting in the sunshine on the terrace with a sandwich (very large one) and a croque monsieur with a cold beer.

We tried after lunch to get a good photograph of the sunflower field that we could see from our bed-room window but the sun wouldn't quite play the game and strangely the flower heads were facing away from the sun. Confused plants. I went back to our friend at the wine shop who we had met in the early morning and had a tasting, buying some of the local Vezaley Chardonnay which is not too dissimilar to Chablis and I am sure could be passed off as such once decanted. Won't do it however. It is not a lot cheaper than Chablis anyway but it was a very fine wine. There is also a really excellent homewares shop on the main route up to the Basilica. This is quite unusual as most of the goods on display are outside in a lovely courtyard that has fantastic views across the valley below. It was strange to our English eyes to see so much fine pottery and decorative items sold in such an outdoor setting but very pleasant and effective it is. We bought some lovely heart shaped dessert plates and also for reasons I cannot explain a small decorative chicken for a present.

Thoughts turned to dinner and we had our eye on two restaurants, one that was open for the first time tonight during the time we were staying here in Vézelay. This had an interesting menu and we possibly also considered the restaurant at the hotel next to ours that had a less interesting menu but lovely white tablecloths. As we went to cast our eye over that menu once again a middle aged man arrived with three elderly people, presumably his parents/in laws. They were all in their 80's having great difficulty getting out of the car and walking down to the restaurant that was serving early evening drinks at that time. It was obviously the man's special treat for them. The lady at the restaurant clearly observed all this but as they reached the terrace she came out with a sign saying 'bar ferme' and turned them away saying they could get a drink at our hotel next door. We thought that was very poorly done as she was still serving customers already there and it did put us off dining there in the evening.

We went out refreshed and all dressed up for a final evening in France but found our first choice fully booked and strangely virtually everywhere else was shut – except our disastrous restaurant from the night before. We didn't want to take the car out into the countryside and were still not inspired by the menu or ambiance next door so decided to simply go and have an ice cream, walk up to the Basilica and buy some snacks and a bottle of chilled Vezaley white wine and have a picnic in the square.

I have to ask though, and not for the first time in Burgundy – Why are so many restaurants ignoring the volume of people around and just taking days off? I think because it probably the start of the French holiday period we have found it quieter than normal but even so it has been VERY quiet indeed.

A funny end to our trip but a most enjoyable one nonetheless as we watched a very gorgeous sunset over the valley and finished a beautiful chilled bottle of local white wine.

It was time to leave France for home and what an enjoyable stay it has been at the Hotel Compostelle following on from our brilliant time in Provence. It is a hotel that in some ways shouldn't really leave you feeling so good about it. The room was basic, some areas of the hotel really need a refit and are tired looking and to some visitors (and possibly I include myself) on first impressions it would make you turn away and run. But what a super place this is. I said it was clean and that is always a big plus but the lovely management and staff have created a very authentic, relaxed and generous atmosphere where nothing is too much trouble and very soon you end up revelling in the very Frenchness of it, warts and all. A happy place.

One final walk around the village and off we went. Burgundy has delighted and infuriated in equal measure but its quietness had done its work and we go home even more chilled than we were when we left Provence.

One last stop was to pull off the auto route near Bethune and head a few miles towards the Belgium border to the small town of La Bassee. During some family history research over the last few years we had discovered that Niamh's great grandfather had been wounded in this area and evacuated home at the start of the First World War and we wanted to have a look.

It was interesting to get a feel for the layout of the town and to see the Canal area that contained a lot of the fighting but a proper look would need more time and we had not got that time available just now. I cannot see the area being on a list of places for a holiday as to be honest it is a bit grim along the road to Lille so perhaps we can give it more time on our next passing through stage.

Again as we found in a lesser sense in Provence that it is very difficult to get your head round the appalling carnage of the area on such a brief visit. Niamh's grandmother was born about a year after his return from France as an invalid so quite a poignant visit as for her if his wounding had not occurred here she would certainly never have been born. Doing the family history makes you appreciate the fine margins there are in making up the family tree. I have since that visit written a book about the family experiences themed around their exploits in various conflicts and enjoyed the research that went into it.

Anyway enough philosophy and soon a dose of

English reality will assault the senses. Could always turn round and head back to Provence. Don't tempt me!

Looking back over the many visits we have made to Provence I am always surprised at just how much we have been able to see and experience. The many people we have met along the way and the variety of emotions that Provence has brought out in us seem disproportionate to the amount of time we have spent there. Provence is a truly magical place and I am glad that we embraced everything we found in that region and did not just sit in a chair in a sunny Gite garden for two weeks but got out to enjoy all that this stunning land has to offer. Yes, we did sit at times, often on a restaurant terrace having a long lunch with a beautiful rosé wine but Provence always seems to open doors to meet new people and find new sights, sounds and fragrances.

I do hope I have inspired you to visit and by all means follow some of our places we have enjoyed but most of all settle into its character and trust your judgement, make choices and find a joy of travel that becomes your very own.

Thank you for reading and I do hope
that you have enjoyed my second book
about our Travels in France

Please note as the purchaser you can download
this book FREE of charge to your Kindle

If you have then please leave a review on
Amazon and follow my Author page to be kept
informed about the next books in the series

My passion is writing about travel and particularly French travel. I have traveled extensively in France and wine and food has always featured on my travels and now in my books. My friends always await our return from France with the latest new finds from the vineyards and I was more than happy to keep sampling. I am from Lancashire in the north of England but have now relocated to Somerset (nearer to France) and able to enjoy devoting my time to writing and new discoveries.

France came late to me as a destination, in fact so conservative was my travel upbringing that it was a long time before I even ventured to Devon or Cornwall. I have more than made up for the slow start and have enjoyed helping many others over the years with their travel plans to France and especially to Paris and Provence.

I have also written about ancestry and genealogy from a military perspective and my book is now available on Amazon.

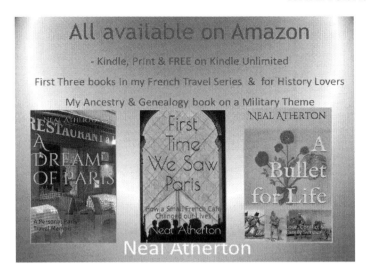

Printed in Great Britain
by Amazon

33094178R00147